PRACTICING HAPPINESS

A MEMOIR OF VAN LIFE

SARAH WYNDE

ROZELLE
PRESS

Published by Rozelle Press
independent publisher of unexpected fiction
and apparently now some non-fiction, too
how unexpected

To the members of the Travato Owners and Wannabes group:
the moderators who keep the conversations focused and civil;
the experienced hands who answer the tough questions;
and the dreamers, who were the inspiration for these pages.
I hope to see you all on the road someday!

INTRODUCTION

In March of 2016, I decided to sell my house, buy a van and travel the country.

I was a single mom whose sole chick had flown the nest; living in Florida in a house I adored but whose upkeep and maintenance were a constant churn of worry in my head; and I was a little less than gainfully employed.

Nomadland hadn't been published yet, and I'd never heard of #vanlife. I didn't even have an Instagram account. But my life felt stagnant. I didn't know what I wanted, but I knew I needed something different.

Of course, if you'd known me back then, you might have said, "Wait. Aren't you clinically agoraphobic? Don't you think that might make living on the road challenging?"

To which I probably would have responded, "Well, yeah. And maybe."

Based on my blog posts and journals, interspersed with some present day advice on van living and happiness, this is the story of what I did, how I did it, and what I learned along the way.

I

BRAVE AND CRAZY

1

HOW IT BEGAN

I started writing my blog ten years ago today.

Time is strange.

Yep, that's my deep, profound, thoughtful cliché on this anniversary of a decade gone by.

I wouldn't have expected the day to be meaningful to me. It's like remembering the anniversary of buying a journal, or maybe a kitchen appliance. Like, "Whoa, this is the ten year anniversary of my electric kettle — I sure have made a lot of tea over the years."

I won't notice the ten year anniversary of my electric kettle and I have no idea why I remembered this anniversary, except that I saw the archive list and realized March 2006 was the earliest date in it.

But ten years is actually a remarkable amount of life.

Ten years ago, I lived in Santa Cruz, with no intention of moving. I'm fairly sure we were living in a run-down, mold-ridden rental house where my bedroom window was permanently cracked to let an electric cord through to the sump pump under the house, and if we weren't living there yet, we were about to be.

Ten years ago, my son had recently been diagnosed as having

severe learning disabilities. Ten years ago, I had a job that paid me well for work I was good at and felt stifled by. Ten years ago, I had an adorable puppy who I already loved with all my heart.

If you'd said to me ten years ago, "What's your life going to be like in ten years?" and then, "What do you want your life to be like in ten years?" I would have answered with, "I have no idea," followed by, "I have no idea."

But if you had said to me back then that in ten years, I'd be living in a cute three-bedroom house in Florida with a window seat and French doors leading to a patio with a swimming pool; that my son would be in college, with multiple scholarships, on the verge of presenting at his second academic conference; that I would be eking out a precarious living by writing fiction; and that the adorable puppy would still be as adorable and would have an adorable companion, I would have laughed at you.

That set of fantasies would have seemed as unrealistic as they come, with the second dog pushing the whole thing over the edge into "Haha, ridiculous."

And yet here we are. Here I am. That is my reality, or at least a window on it.

For some reason, it makes me want to cry. I wish I could go back to that self, who was always tired, and often depressed, being made sick, sick, sicker by the mold in that horrible house, and tell her what the future would bring.

Not that it didn't bring plenty of bad along with the good — these ten years have held more grief and loss than I could have handled knowing about back then.

But it's amazing to me to look around at my life, to think about the friends I hadn't even met yet, the knowledge I didn't have, and realize how far I've come, how much I've changed.

The thing about looking back on ten years, though, is that it also inspires me to look forward.

Where do I want to be ten years from now?

What do I want out of the next ten years of my life?

I got here by taking chances. By doing things that seemed impulsive and scary. Moving to Florida was huge; quitting my job even bigger; dropping out of graduate school terrifying (and yet still the right call, I think).

What terrifying things do I want to do in the next ten years?

Five days ago, I thought, "Maybe I should sell the house and buy an RV. It could be my tiny, mobile house. I could live in it with the dogs, write just the way I do here, cook in my tiny kitchen, and drive around the country looking for beautiful sunsets."

Four days ago, I started telling people — my dad, my brother, my friend Tim — that I was thinking about it.

Three days ago, I started researching RVs.

Two days ago, I started cleaning out my garage and closets.

Yesterday, I called a realtor.

Today, I'm making it real. I've decided. I'm going to embark on the biggest adventure of my life. It's exciting and terrifying and exciting again.

Getting rid of all of my things is going to be hard and painful and take forever; selling the house will simultaneously be freeing and agonizing; the process of buying an RV frightens me like nothing I've done since buying a house; and it will be ever so strange when R has a school break and I offer him a tent to sleep in.

But ten years from now, I want to look back and think, "Wow, you might have been crazy, but you sure were brave."

MARCH 19, 2016

By 8:58 AM, I had burned myself on hot oil, cut myself on a can, and stepped on something sharp, either a tiny piece of glass or a thorn. When I turned around too fast and hit my elbow on my vacuum cleaner, I knew it was probably time to go back to bed.

But I have a belief that keeps me going on days like today — the earthquake theory of karma. Basically, when lots of little things are going wrong, I think it's the universe's way of bleeding off your bad luck, like the tiny earthquakes that alleviate stress on a fault line and prevent a major earthquake from happening.

So when I'm poking at my foot, trying to figure out what just caused that drop of blood and whether it's still in there, I'm trying to remember to be grateful that I'm not going to get in a car accident today or drop dead from a heart attack or experience whatever big bad luck might have been headed my way.

Yes, I know it's ridiculous. But it's still comforting.

And I'm feeling the need of comforting. I keep reminding myself that this is my choice, my decision, and I can change my mind if I want to.

But the fun part of my adventure is a long way away. I'm currently in the stressful part of deciding what needs to be done before I can put the house on the market, and what I'm going to keep and how.

I've done this kind of major purge before, but not nearly as extreme as I'm planning now. When I moved from California to Florida, I got rid of everything — or rather, everything that didn't have sentimental value. That's an important distinction.

In the ten years since, I've gained lots of stuff, some of it just from living, which is easy to let go of if tedious to go through, but plenty of it with sentimental value.

I look around my room. There's a porcelain centaur sitting on my bookcase. I bought it in Spain when I was 17 years old. It lived in my parents' house until my mom died, but now I have it. Am I getting rid of it?

In the corner is a Beanie Baby hedgehog, one of the only stuffed animals left from when R was that age. He had dozens, of course, as kids do, but they're all gone, except for this little hedgehog that's been keeping me company for the past decade. Can I say good-bye to it?

In front of it, a tile with R's five-year-old handprint. How can I possibly toss that out?

And on, and on, and on, it goes.

I'm trying to balance my competing needs — to take my time looking through it and to get rid of it all as quickly and painlessly as possible. To save what I value but not get bogged down in owning (or being owned by) a lot of things. To respect my past but not wallow in it.

It's strange to drag all of your past out into the light and examine it, though. Trying to decide what to keep, what should go, what matters, what doesn't.

I keep reminding myself that I don't have to be in a rush, but I'd like to move on to the fun part of this big adventure.

APRIL 11, 2016

The sweet olive tree outside my bedroom window is in full bloom. It has deep green leaves and little white flowers and it smells incredible, exotic and tropical and somehow warm.

I ate outside this morning, watching the bees start to buzz around the tree, admiring the bright flowers on the (evil) bougainvillea, listening to the birds, and thought, "Am I crazy? How can I let this go?"

But it only took me a second to remind myself that the tree doesn't bloom year-round, that the patio needs pressure-washing to get rid of the mold, that the pool should really be re-surfaced sometime soon, even though my new (expensive) variable-speed pool pump is doing an awesome job, and that I'm guaranteed the occasional beautiful morning in a life on the road, even if many of them wind up being views of concrete pads and other RVs.

It was reassuring.

In yoga today, L, the yoga instructor, read a beautiful piece about non-attachment to objects. So fitting. I tried to find it online so I could share it, but she told me to google "yamas" and there's so much info out there that I can't find the right poem. Or prayer. Maybe it was both. Either way, it was perfectly timed.

APRIL 18, 2016

The painters are here. By the end of today or maybe tomorrow, the whole house will be a subtle gray.

It's a nice color, but I'm not sure how I feel about it. It's strange to be making the house nice so that I can (eventually) hand the keys over to someone else. The last few days I've been cleaning everything, taking down the pictures, stacking up the books in boxes in the garage or piles in my closet.

I should take a photo of my closet because the piles are ridiculous. I started by putting just a few books in there. The ones that might be essential, the ones that maybe I couldn't get rid of. And then the books that were meaningful.

Not the ones that were so meaningful that there was no way I was getting rid of them. That tiny collection made it into my mom's cedar chest to get stored in my brother's basement. When I'm 80 years old and living in an assisted living facility, I'll be using a magnifying glass to read the copy of *Winnie the Pooh* my parents gave me for my fourth birthday or the copy of *The White Dragon* that was an unexpected gift in sixth grade.

But the others.

The *Hunger Games* trilogy, because when the third book released, R came home from school to find me reading it. Every twenty minutes for the next two hours he came into my room and said, "Aren't you done yet?" until finally, exasperated, I said, "Do you need me to go to Barnes & Noble and buy another copy so you can start reading it now?"

He said, "Yes."

He said yes!

My dyslexic boy, who I was told might never be able to read, couldn't wait two hours longer to get his hands on *Mockingjay*. Do I need to keep the whole trilogy for that? Probably not. But the sight of the books spurs the memory and the memory brings me joy.

Some Dianna Wynne Jones books. They were the first books I bought for myself. I've carted them from place to place for decades, keeping them even when letting go of so many others. The complete works of Lois McMaster Bujold, comfort food when I'm sick. Some cookbooks: the *Zuni Cafe* cookbook that taught me so much, the

Smitten Kitchen cookbook that my aunt gave me, the *Perfect Recipe* cookbook that I use every Thanksgiving.

These are not books that are going to fit in an RV.

Maybe I stick them in a box and let them live in my brother's basement for a while, waiting for the day I decide on a new home base. Or maybe I give them to friends, trying to find them new homes with people who might love them. Or maybe I donate them to the library, letting chance and fate decide whether some stranger discovers something that delights them or whether they wind up in a landfill.

It was just about a month ago that I decided to embark on this adventure. I remind myself regularly, almost daily, that I can change my mind. This is my decision, my choice. If it's too hard, I don't have to do it.

But underneath all the fear and all the angst about things, objects, stuff, a drumbeat of excitement steadily thumps away. I have no idea what the future is going to bring, but letting go of the past is the first step on the path to finding out.

Someday, sooner rather than later, I'm going to eat a lobster in Maine, go grocery shopping in South Dakota, admire the Grand Canyon with my own eyes, and watch the sun rise over a beach while I walk the dogs before settling down to write.

But first I have to let go of these books.

ON CHOOSING & BUYING AN RV

When I decided to move into an RV, my experience with them consisted of traveling with my parents when I was younger and one — yes, exactly one! — trip taken in a borrowed 30-foot Class C.

Although I didn't write about it at the time, I dived into the research. I bought books on RVs, investigated reliability and safety, checked consumer reports, read blogs and reviews, and visited multiple dealers over the course of several weeks.

My early assumption was that I'd be looking for a used Class C. Used, because they're the best deal. Class C, because after all, I was going to be living in it. It needed to have enough room for me and my two dogs, 24/7.

The more I looked, though, the more I felt drawn to the Class B's, aka the camper vans. Most of them were out of my price range, however, and some of them felt so much like metal boxes that I couldn't imagine spending my days inside one.

I rejected the first Class B I went inside immediately. Dark and gloomy, I thought. I went back to the Class Cs, narrowing my search down to the 24-foot models.

But then I went inside a Winnebago Travato 59K. The floor plan is simple: bathroom in the back, then two twin beds that can convert into a double bed, then a kitchen with a sink, a two-burner stove, and a half-size refrigerator. The driver and passenger seats rotate to form a seating area. And it's got lots of windows, making for great light.

It felt fun.

It also felt flexible. At 20 feet long, it's small enough to park in a normal parking spot or a driveway. At the time, I didn't imagine I'd be spending a lot of time in driveways, but I knew I wanted to visit people and I thought a Travato would make that easier than a bigger RV.

Also, I admit, I was kind of intimidated by the bigger RVs. I knew I could drive one — I'd done it before — but I wasn't sure I really wanted to. When I drove a Travato for the first time, it felt like driving a mini-van.

At that moment, I made the decision. Van life it would be. (I hadn't actually heard of #vanlife at the time: months later, someone sent me an article about it and I learned how trendy I was being.)

Back then, Travatos were fairly new on the market and there weren't many used ones for sale, so I wound up buying a new one off the lot from a nearby dealer.

If I went back in time, I'd probably make all the same decisions. They weren't bad decisions, based on the knowledge I had and the constraints I was working with.

But if you're considering making a similar purchase, I strongly suggest looking for people having online conversations — Facebook groups and the like — and finding out what other people have paid for your prospective vehicle and what issues concern them.

Specifically, the *Travato Owners and Wannabes* group on Facebook is a fantastic resource. I found them after I bought my van, but I suspect I could have saved several thousand dollars if I'd found them a few weeks sooner.

JUNE 23, 2016

When I woke up this morning, I had a moment of thinking, "Thursday, must blog, what am I going to write about?" and then I thought, "Duh."

Seriously, it was a very half-awake thought because in reality I'm bubbling over with excitement, wanting to babble my news to anyone who will listen.

Yesterday I bought my RV, a Winnebago Travato 59K.

In that list of adjectives up above, the amusement is because I'm so very, very excited about Serenity. *Oh, the irony.*

Although maybe I should start calling her a camper? The Class B people seem to use camper or van when referring to their homes-on-wheels, Class B being the type of RV I chose.

I'm excited. And scared. And excited again. And overwhelmed and excited and amused and excited and... yeah. I'll stop there.

I haven't gotten to take possession of her yet. It takes the service guys a couple of days to prep her and get her ready and then we do a big walkthrough where I check everything and they teach me everything I need to know.

The walkthrough can take several hours, so I'm not sure when that will happen but not before the weekend, I suppose. Apart from any other issues, I need to arrange for a ride to the dealer, since obviously I'll be driving away in *Serenity*.

Yep, that's her name. It's probably a cliché for geeks to name their vehicles *Serenity*, but I was thinking of doing so anyway — not just for the *Firefly* reference, but for the reminder to myself that serenity is the true destination of my journey.

Then R said, upon seeing a picture, "You must name it *Serenity*." Decision made.

Serenity is, if it's not obvious, very small. Well, relatively speaking. If you're used to driving a Honda Civic, as I am, she feels big. But she's more like a mini-van than a classic sleeping-area-over-the-cab RV. And storage is going to be tight, even tighter than I imagined.

When I was looking at the overhead compartments yesterday and the depth of the drawers, I quailed. But just for a moment.

There's not going to be any bringing along of stuff "just in case" and I'm going to have to make some hard decisions. I'm going from a pantry the size of a full-length bedroom closet to one cabinet, the size of maybe half an overhead airplane bin. From a full-size refrigerator and freezer to a dorm-room size fridge. From a walk-in closet to a tiny wardrobe with a couple drawers beneath it. It sounds impossible.

And so, so, so exciting!

JUNE 27, 2016

I woke up a while back to the sound of ticking. Not a big sound, a little sound. *Tick, tick, tick.*

My first sleepy thought was, "I should get rid of that clock. I don't need more things to ruin my sleep."

My second sleepy thought was, "I don't have a clock."

From sleepy to heart-racing in two seconds.

My thoughts went like this: there's a ticking noise. I don't own a clock. It must be a bomb. There's a bomb in my bedroom. Someone must have stolen into my room and planted a bomb under my bed. They want to blow me up because... nope. That's silly. There's no reason anyone would want to blow me up.

Okay, then it's not a bomb. It must be a watch. Someone's standing in my room watching me sleep and wearing a watch. A burglar?

Tick, tick, tick

Although wouldn't my dogs make some noise if a stranger was in my room? If I can startle them by setting my coffee cup down too hard, how are they sleeping through an unknown person wandering around?

Finally I opened my eyes. My fan was on. The *tick* was the cord, gently banging on the base.

I find this to be a cautionary tale about my own tendency to jump to the worst possible conclusions. Lately, whenever my brain gets stuck worrying about something I can't control, I remind myself that it's probably not a bomb.

JULY 4, 2016

I picked *Serenity* up last Wednesday. Yay!

That night, she was sitting in my driveway, feeling something like an overwhelming Christmas present, needing to be unwrapped but almost too scary to touch.

SARAH WYNDE

So much to learn, so much to do, so much stuff to move in and organize and...

...that all became irrelevant Thursday evening, when in the midst of a torrential rainstorm, I discovered that it was also raining inside *Serenity*.

I'm trying to view this as fortunate. It happened while I was here, still with a dry bed to sleep in. It happened in a big way. If the weather hadn't been so extreme, it might have taken me weeks to realize that a few drips were a symptom of a serious problem. It happened before I'd moved much stuff into her, so she could go back to the dealer without inconveniencing me unduly.

All good things.

Of course, they're counter-balanced by the rather bad thing of it raining inside my future home, but hey, glass half-full. I would have been very unhappy to learn that she leaked at 3AM when I was sleeping under the leak.

So, yeah, *Serenity* is back at the dealer and I'm hoping to get her back sometime this week.

Meanwhile, the house is a mess and I still need to get rid of more stuff. I'm definitely at the point where the decisions get harder and harder.

Also much trying to plan. The house closes three weeks from today. Where am I going to sleep that night?

JULY 11, 2016

R came home for the weekend, which was lovely.

We went out for sushi at our favorite sushi place on Friday night. On Saturday, we ran some errands: another load of stuff to Goodwill and also a run to the storage unit. On Sunday, he woke up late, then went out to lunch with a friend. When he came home, we watched *Interstellar*. Afterwards, he helped me drag some stuff out to the curb — his box spring and mattress, an old washing machine that's been in the garage for the past seven years.

We talked about his trip to Ireland and his job, his thoughts for the future, ideas about plays he's writing and his thesis, places he wants to go, and the movies we were watching. A show he's watching on Netflix that I would hate but that makes him laugh. *Game of Thrones*, which neither of us watch, but both of us know too much about.

We put *Serenity*'s name on her. He'd been joking about my spaceship since he first saw her, but when he looked at the name lettering I'd gotten, he told me I'd picked a very Christian font.

I was a little taken aback, but he viewed this as a good thing. He said when I was broken down by the side of the road, people would be inspired to want to help me.

And then he got into his car and drove away. And I will not see him again until 2017. And we will probably never live in the same house again.

I am so sad. Also now completely congested, eyes puffy, face tear-stained, and sick of crying.

Change happens. It's not always easy. This change is better for me than sitting in this house, waiting for him to visit, so I know it's right.

But a little grieving, that's right, too.

JULY 14, 2016

I have this vexing, nagging sense of worry, the feeling of Stuff To Be Done, like I need to make to-do lists and organize and do ALL the things.

But that sense is actually what my problem is. Not that I need to do ALL the things, because really, I don't. There's plenty of time to do what needs doing.

The problem is the anxiety that leads to me thinking I need to do ALL the things. The anxiety gets in the way of enjoying the day I'm in, of feeling joy, of being able to free up my mind and my imagination for the life that I want to live instead of the anxiety that I'm choosing to live in. And anxiety is a choice, even though it doesn't feel like one.

I need to remember to step back and see it as a choice and then stop making that choice in whatever way works. Yoga, maybe, at least when it's not turning into something else on the Anxiety Life List of Things that Should Be Done.

I wonder if I'll be able to find yoga on the road. Or be comfortable doing yoga in campgrounds? Gah. I already have so many fears that worrying about whether I'll be able to do yoga is just icing on my negativity cake.

JULY 18, 2016

I had an incredibly productive Monday morning:

- I scheduled an appointment at the RV dealer to get *Serenity*'s vent fixed.
- I called the fence people about the permit problem.
- I took a load of stuff to Goodwill, probably the last.
- I stopped at the pharmacy and picked up a prescription and discussed arrangements for refills on the road.
- I called my doctor and got a couple extra refills added to my prescription.
- I took some old cans of paint and bug spray to the landfill.
- I loaded up *Serenity* with four bookcases and a chair and drove them to the house of the friend who's taking them.
- I posted a question about traveling with pets to Facebook.
- I emailed my realtor.
- I called the guy who's taking my porch furniture and made arrangements with him for Thursday.
- I talked to my sister and set up a time for my nephew to come collect a few things.
- I spent some time researching temperature monitoring solutions for when I have to leave the dogs in *Serenity*.*

And then I sat down at the computer to work and... didn't. Someday soon, I have to get back to trying to earn a living. Meanwhile, though, a week from today, I'll be on the road, headed to Pennsylvania, and all the house-related to-do list items will be done. I don't know whether I'm more relieved, scared, or excited.

*The temperature inside *Serenity* hit 122 degrees the other day. I was impressed. That was with all windows closed and no air-conditioning on, of course, on a Florida day in July — a situation in which I would never leave the dogs. But I would like some kind of warning system for when I do leave them, although preferably one that doesn't cost a small fortune.

JULY 21, 2016

I spent a couple hours this morning moving into *Serenity*. Like, really moving into *Serenity*.

Tomorrow morning when I want coffee, it'll be in the van. When I get dressed, I'll be running out to the driveway first. My cooking capability in my house is down to... well, nothing, actually. My frying pan and two pots are both in the van, along with all my utensils.

Does this make any sense? Answer: Nope.

I've got four more days in my house and *Serenity*'s not hooked up to water, and the refrigerator's not cold, so it's impractical to think I can really just stay in her.

But I've been having to make tough choices about what I can and can't bring and tomorrow is my last trash day, so I needed to make decisions. The easiest way to decide was to try things out.

It was fun. I put all my dishes and pantry goods onto the shelves, then realized that when the bed is made up as a double bed instead of two singles, one of the cabinets will be difficult to access.

So I rearranged everything. Then I decided that my shelves didn't work the way I needed them to, so I did it again. It felt like playing house, like being a little kid in a pretend kitchen, doing pretend shopping.

JULY 23, 2016

I slept in the house last night, but this morning I decided to have my first meal in *Serenity*. I brought my milk, my cereal and a nectarine out to the driveway and made myself a cup of coffee while I sliced up the nectarine.

I sat on the edge of the van, the sliding door open, coffee on the floor next to me, bowl of cereal in my hand, adoring dogs at my feet.

A bird was flitting in and out of my crepe myrtle tree, which is in full, gorgeous pink bloom, and the sky was the pure blue of early morning with some wispy white clouds floating by.

I took a deep breath and thought about how a peaceful morning just sets the tone for the whole day.

And then a dog walked by and Zelda went berserk and I grabbed for her brand-new tie-out cord, throwing my cereal into the air.

Before we were through, I had nectarine and milk and soggy rice Chex in my coffee and on the floor and even on the comforter on the bed next to the door.

Yeah, that happened.

I didn't let either dog lick up the milk and cereal, and I growled at Zelda as I cleaned up the mess. Literally, a low rumble of annoyance.

Still, I've got a definite glow of joy going.

JULY 25, 2016

Yesterday was a perfect day. Not just a nice day, not just a good day, but an authentically perfect day.

I'd been dreading it for weeks. My last full day in my house, my last moment to say good-bye. I expected loneliness and sorrow, regret and probably some worry about the future.

Instead, I puttered around, moving stuff from one place to another. I went for a walk with a friend, cleaned, saw another friend, ran some errands. Spent half an hour on the phone with R, made lunch, cleaned some more, went out and saw some other friends, made dinner.

About 9, when I was tired and ready to sleep, I came back into the house. I went out to the swimming pool and lit the torches and swam by firelight under a starry sky.

It was so beautiful. I floated in the still water, watching the colors of the flames against the backdrop of the leafy bamboo. The sweet olive tree was even blooming again, making the whole backyard smell tropical. It was as magical as I could have imagined.

The only not quite perfect thing was that poor Zelda was so tired from staying two inches away from me while I wandered around that when I swam she didn't play with her ball. Instead she slept, as if she was grateful for the chance to get some rest while I was contained. She, of course, doesn't know that it's going to be her last chance to play in a pool for a while.

And today's the big day. I suspect that it is both going to fly by and have long moments where it feels like it's dragging, but at 2 PM, I will sign the papers.

One set of dreams will come to an end, but another will begin.

2

GETTING STARTED

Yesterday was a whirlwind, but eventually, I was on the highway, *Serenity* and I heading north, and two things were happening.

First, my brain wasn't letting go of house worries. I kept trying to convince myself that it was finally my chance to think about my writing, but my brain just would not unlock.

And second, I could feel myself getting driven to reach Pennsylvania. I was tired, my back was sore, I was hungry, but I just kept going. As if I was going to make it to Pennsylvania in the next two hours.

Given that my destination is 800 miles away and that there's no reason for me to get there before Thursday, I knew I was being stupid. Well, or rather High Persistence, which is one of my character traits that's always been both a blessing and a curse. Eventually I pulled over in a rest stop, found a place to stay, called to check availability, and wound up at St. Johns RV.

It's nothing special, just your basic field with concrete pads. But there are some trees and a nice long walk for the dogs. Both of them refused to come back into *Serenity* this morning after their walk, so I got a chance to try out their brand-new tie-out lines. Zelda promptly wound herself around the tree. Ha. It'll take practice, I expect, since they've never been tied up before.

Still, it's getting hot already — not quite 9, and it's 86 degrees inside *Serenity* — so it's probably time to get on the road. I don't wish I was staying because *Serenity* is filled with stuff that I'm taking to my brother's house, but I'm looking forward to the day when my goal isn't to get on the road, but to enjoy where I am. Soon!

JULY 26, 2016 - DILLON, SOUTH CAROLINA

376 miles today. I don't intend to have days like this often. I kept passing places that sounded intriguing and wanting to stop: historical sites and parks, beaches and artisan stores. But I just kept driving by. The point of my adventurous life is not to always be moving.

Well, sort of it is, but not moving without stopping at the cool stuff along the way. Once I get to Pennsylvania and unload the things that are making life in *Serenity* complicated — she's not sized for carrying Christmas ornaments, my mom's china, and a large-screen television — I'm going to be slowing way down. When I see something that sounds fun, I will stop.

Not, however, when it's a restaurant. What is it about road trips that makes unhealthy food seem so appealing? I wanted waffles today. And pancakes. McDonald's french fries. Fried chicken. BBQ. Every time I saw a sign for a restaurant I'd never heard of, I wanted to stop and check it out, and every time I saw a sign for fast food that I once liked and haven't eaten in years, I also wanted to stop.

I wasn't even hungry most of the time. For breakfast, I had rice Chex with fresh blueberries. For lunch, prosciutto-wrapped dates and cherries. For dinner, turkey slices rolled up with peach-honey mustard, avocado, and arugula inside, with sliced radishes as a side. How could McDonald's compare? And yet...

One of the reasons I drove so far today was that it's uncomfortably hot. I thought about stopping earlier, but with the van moving, both dogs were in the front seat area, air-conditioning blasting on them, as the back got hotter and hotter. I knew if we stopped in the heat of the day, the AC would be hard-pressed to keep up.

It can drop the temperature about 20 degrees, I think, less if the van's sitting in full sun. With temperatures breaking 100, stopping earlier would have meant sitting inside an 80 degree van, at best, or staying outside in the heat. I could have done it and Zelda probably would have been fine, but poor Bartleby has thick black fur and does not love the heat.

I accidentally gave B a full Benadryl tonight. I don't know what I was thinking — over-tired, I guess — but I stuck the whole pill in the peanut butter and handed it to him and only thought, "Oh, wait, I usually cut it in half," when it was already in his mouth. Not like I could get it back at that point, but I was filled with maternal anxiety.

Not about whether it would be bad for him — a double-dose of Benadryl's not going to kill him — but about whether his reaction would be stoned dog or hyper dog. Either was possible. I'm feeling exceedingly fortunate that his eyes are glazed and his head nodding. I should probably drag him out for a last walk before he completely crashes, though.

INTRODUCING THE DOGS

In 2005, family friends gave us a Jack Russell terrier puppy. We named her Zelda, after the princess from the *Legend of Zelda* games. She was supposed to be my son's dog, but that lasted for about fifteen minutes, and then she was mine, body and soul. I worked at home and she was my constant companion.

Like all Jack Russells, she was active, independent, and amazingly intelligent. She was my first dog and I didn't have the perspective to understand how smart she was until I'd had some exposure to other dogs and realized she was brilliant. She was also incredibly sweet-natured. She had one priority in life: the care and protection of me, her person.

I have hundreds of pictures of the dogs, but remarkably few where they're conveniently posing together.

In 2013, an overweight, scruffy, long-haired chihuahua mix wandered into my (fully-fenced!) backyard and settled down for a nap on Zelda's dog bed. After searching for his owners and taking him to the vet, we concluded that someone had dumped him. He had an assortment of health problems: skin conditions, allergies, bad joints, elevated liver enzymes, and eventually the symptoms of congestive heart failure. He'd also obviously not had an easy life — he spent most of his first year with me hiding in my closet.

I had no intention of getting a second dog, and I would never have picked a long-haired chihuahua if I had, but Bartleby stole my heart. He loved to snuggle, loved to be petted, adored small children. He was not exactly a good dog: he was quick to snap if scared and he drew my blood more than once when I had to do something he didn't appreciate (i.e., cleaning his ears when he had an ear infection.) But I loved him and eventually he loved me.

You may have noticed that I'm using the past tense. I hate, hate, HATE books where the dog dies. For me, that's an absolutely fine reason to throw a book across the room and refuse to read anymore.

But SPOILERS: this book is about my real life, not fiction, and real life isn't always easy.

Yes, both dogs will die. Yes, I will grieve. In fact, I'm crying as I write this, because it's such a reminder of how much I love them and how much I miss them.

Before that happens, though, we will have many cautious adventures and we will practice much happiness. And I hope that you, dear reader, will be brave enough to continue this journey with us, even knowing what you now know.

JULY 28, 2016 - SOMEWHERE IN NORTH CAROLINA

I had an adventure!

Although I admit, as adventures go, this one was pretty tame. It took place mostly in my imagination. But in my imagination, it was loads of fun.

I was at a rest stop on 95, in North Carolina. It was around lunchtime, so early. I'd walked the dogs already, enjoying the feeling of forest, the humidity in the air that felt heavier and damper than Florida humidity.

I liked it. Wouldn't want to stay in it forever, because the bugs liked it, too, but it was fun to feel the sensation of being in a different climate.

I was looking at campgrounds on my phone. A Thousand Trails campground, Lake Gaston RV, looked nice. It was still in North Carolina, only 45 minutes away, so it meant a short day, followed by a long day tomorrow, but a quiet afternoon on a lake sounded appealing.

Decision made, I made a reservation, called up the GPS on my phone and headed out while my phone considered the route.

Lesson learned: make sure to have the directions **before** getting on the highway. For some reason, my phone got very confused. It wanted me to "proceed to the route." I would have loved to, if I had any idea how.

For about five minutes, at 70mph, it told me that I was 600 feet away from my route. That had to be a lie. And then it decided I was still in Florida. It would have been a fine time to have a navigator to figure out what the heck was going on, but neither Zelda nor Bartleby seemed interested in taking on the job.

So I got off the highway and looked for a place to park to figure out what I was doing.

Um, note to self: *Serenity* is taller than a Honda Civic. I drove under some trees that scraped along the top, got flustered, wound up in some mud, couldn't get the phone to work, had cars whizzing by...

Finally I used the navigation system built-in to *Serenity*. It told me to turn around. I made a cautious K turn, hurrying and anxious, and headed out.

For the first ten miles, the drive was lovely. It was so nice to be off the highway. 95 creates the illusion that the whole country is exactly alike, McDonald's and Shell stations and asphalt.

Sure, the billboards advertise peaches and pecans in Georgia, but mostly one mile is the same as the next. Driving along a road of fields and little brick houses was much more interesting. Slow, but that was okay. I wasn't in a hurry.

Then the line on the map I was following told me to turn. Obedient to the whims of my electronic guide, I did.

Onto a dirt and gravel road that led to a tiny bridge signposted with weight warnings. What? According to the numbers, I was still 20 miles away from my destination. Could this really be the road?

I hadn't intended to go hours out of my way. The original map had made it look as if the campground was about twenty minutes off the highway. I was already at least twenty minutes away from the highway.

But I drove onto the dirt road. It was exactly like you'd think it would be — bumpy and rough and kicking up a cloud of dust as I puttered along at about ten miles per hour.

And suddenly I knew where I was — in the beginning of a romance novel. When the photographer or journalist or whatever she is — not quite Too Stupid To Live, but maybe borderline — follows bad directions and winds up on the farm owned by the good-looking curmudgeon with the heart of gold.

Except, no blizzard. In a romance novel, I would be destined to get trapped on the farm and that means blizzard. No blizzard, no romance.

Okay, so maybe I was in a thriller. I follow the wrong road and see something mysterious. Maybe two suspicious men exchanging an envelope. They'd see me, too, and then I'd be in danger. Strange men would start following me, a car with heavily tinted windows would try to force me off the road.

Except there was nothing on this road but me in a cloud of dirt and lots of green leaves and trees.

So maybe I was in a horror movie. The forest had a great vibe for that — beautiful, innocent, flourishing. What darkness might it be hiding? I'd be trapped on the road, lost, and I'd go up to the spooky house, the one with the porch that creaked.

But we didn't have enough characters for a horror movie. Plus, dogs. Who would write a horror movie with dogs in it? Bartleby would not be a good horror movie victim — he's just too pitiful, especially right now when he's been chewing off his fur. And Zelda might be a good character in a horror movie — she'd be the dog barking furiously at nothing — but I would never ignore her if she were barking furiously. I'd pay attention. We'd leave. End of movie in the first act.

That left murder mystery. And sadly, the only way that storyline made sense was if I was the victim. The innocent shower taker at the Bates Motel; the empty van still running, abandoned in a field; the body washed up on a beach. The story would open with me, but then jump to the world-weary detective, burned out on the job but determined to solve this one last case, the greatest of their career.

And then the dirt road came to an end and I was back on a normal road, pretty much highway-ish, wandering through a small town, and eventually deposited neatly at the front of a campground.

There's a pool, a gorgeous lake, loads of people, a tiny restaurant that looks out on the lake; golf carts and pine trees and red-clay dirt that thrills me because it's not Florida dirt, not New York dirt, not Californian dirt. Not, in other words, dirt that I know.

Adventure over. But fun while it lasted, even though all that happened was that I got lost and wound up on a dirt road.

I made up for my lack of true adventure by braving my kitchen tonight. I've eaten plenty of cold food — salads and roll-ups and plates of fruit and veggies — but it's been too hot to think turning on a heat source made sense.

But tonight I used both burners of the stove and made rice noodles and salmon. Entirely edible, and both my stove and the hot water heater worked the way they're supposed to. Yay! I like having my adventures be imaginary, not technical.

Now I'm listening to rain on the roof. Loads of rumbling thunder, but it feels quite peaceful inside.

JULY 29, 2016 - ALLENTOWN, PENNSYLVANIA

It's a misty wet morning in Pennsylvania, the kind where the sky is a solid mass of lukewarm gray, not stormy, not cloudy, just overcast. I had my window open last night — for the first time, no air-conditioning running — and it was great, but this morning I discovered water dripping in and running down the wall.

I immediately jumped to full-blown paranoia. Oh, no, water in the RV. She'll grow mold and delaminate and the walls will fall apart and she'll be unlivable!

And then I took a deep breath and exhaled and actually looked at that wall.

Water in RVs is a big concern for those aforementioned reasons, but *Serenity*'s a camper van, not a classic RV. Her walls are metal and solid plastic, like the kind they make playground equipment out of these days.

She can't possibly delaminate, because her walls aren't made of laminate. True, if I let her cushions stay damp for days, they could grow mold, but obviously, I won't be doing that.

In other words, it's probably not a bomb. I wish my brain did not jump so quickly to worst-case scenarios.

I made it to my brother's house after a ridiculously long day of driving yesterday. I should have stopped at a campground, but I was close enough that I stuck it out. Rainy rush hour driving through a construction zone after nine hours on the road was probably not a good idea, but we got here.

Last night therefore was my first night camping in someone's front yard. This morning after I walked the dogs, I took our empty water jug up to my brother's front door. Locked. So I went around the side of the house, unlatched the fence and found the water spigot in the back yard. I filled up my jug with water, came home and made myself some coffee.

It was ridiculously fun. I'm not sure why: obviously, in mid-winter, if it was cold outside, it would not be entertaining to be hunting down water.

But it's not mid-winter, it's high summer. I had to push aside the branches of an apple tree with little green apples on it to get to the water, walking by beds of strawberry plants, flowering bushes, and what looked like an ocean of squash. The raspberry bushes had a few last berries on them, but mostly I missed my chance at berries this year. Next summer, I'm going to try to make it here in time for the strawberries.

JULY 31, 2016 - ALLENTOWN, PENNSYLVANIA

My Saturday night was an exercise in contrasts.

It started out great. I had a nice day, filled with family time. After dinner, we watched *Guardians of the Galaxy*, and at 10:30, my niece, sister-in-law, and I headed to Barnes & Noble for the big *Harry Potter* release. My niece and I sat at the Ravenclaw table and colored while her mom waited in line.

But when I finally got to bed, *Serenity* smelled.

Bad.

Like something had gone profoundly wrong with the black tank, where the sewage accumulates. I tossed and turned, worrying and sleepless, making plans.

I'd take her to a dump station in the morning. Or no, maybe a full hook-up campground would be better. I hadn't dumped the tanks yet, so I wouldn't want to figure it out with someone waiting in line behind me.

Still, how could the smell have gotten so bad, so fast? Maybe a week in the heat of summer was too much to let accumulate? But I'd mostly been using bathrooms at rest stops and campgrounds and my brother's house. TMI, but there shouldn't have been enough waste in the tank to make it smell so awful.

However, clearly there was, because it was bad.

Really bad.

But it shouldn't be.

But it was.

So was something wrong?

Toss, turn, toss, turn, worry, hold my breath against the smell, try to sleep, toss, turn, worry, repeat endlessly.

At 4AM, Bartleby wanted to go out. Sometime after that, maybe 5ish, Zelda wanted the same. I think I finally fell asleep for a while after the sun came up.

When I did get up, I discovered that the black tank was fine. One of the dogs had had diarrhea under the bed while I was at B&N.

Ugh. So not nice.

And made even worse by worrying about them, of course. B has been scratching himself into a scabby hairless mess and Z has been refusing to eat her kibble. I think both of them will love this lifestyle eventually, but at the moment, they're stressed out.

I stuck to my campground plan, in part to empty the tanks and in part because the house electricity was just about enough to run the AC, but not if I did anything else that took power. Plus, it only worked if I was parked in the driveway, close enough to the house for a single cord to reach *Serenity*, but on a steep slope. The extension cords we had — not the heavy-duty kind — couldn't handle the load when *Serenity* was in the street.

I'm now in a KOA campground about twenty minutes away. It's expensive, but nice. There's mini golf, a swimming pool, a playground, and plenty of grass and trees. The spot I'm in is huge for *Serenity*, with a picnic table and fire pit.

The best part about it is that *Serenity* is backed up to a stream.

Zelda saw the stream and immediately waded right in. B saw the stream and immediately sat down and refused to move any further. So typical!

AUGUST 1, 2016 - ALLENTOWN, PENNSYLVANIA

Sitting in a parking lot outside the vet. Both dogs are inside, getting looked at. Poor Z was frantic about being left, but B, it turns out, had a goopy ear, which inspired me to ask to have Z's ears checked, too.

They'll also give her an exam, so if her stomach stuff is anything feverish, we'll find out about it. Given the circumstances, I'm really not worried that it's anything more than stress. Well, that's not true. I'm worried, but I know it's probably not a bomb.

This morning's walk took place in something between a mist and a drizzle. I could hear the rain in the trees, but it felt like a cool damp breeze on my skin. Like walking in a cloud, but a cloud at a temperature that felt lovely, not too warm, not too cold.

I walked both dogs around the block, so to speak. Is it a loop in a campground? But when we got back to *Serenity*, Z didn't want to go inside, so I left B and took her on more of a hike. We walked up the road, past campers and trailers and sites more like summer homes than temporary habitations, up and up, and then found a trail through the woods that led to the front of the campground.

It was exactly like my daydream of a week ago. Except for the bugs and the sticks that kept getting in my shoes and the drizzle. But the joy and the sense of freedom and adventure, those were exactly right.

3

SETTLING IN

I had another adventure yesterday.

I went to the grocery store.

Yes, that makes me laugh, too. But it sure felt like an adventure. Strange roads, following my GPS, managing the parking lot, running the generator and air-conditioner for the dogs, roaming the aisles of an unfamiliar store. I also stopped at a farm stand, run by a woman in Amish clothing, where I bought shallots, a squash, and a cantaloupe.

I thought about going to a museum. According to Roadtrippers, the Agricultural and Industrial Museum was right down the road from the grocery store. It felt like it would be virtuous to go to the museum, like it was something I should do.

But while I waited for my GPS to give me directions, I remembered two things.

First, I'm not a tourist. My goal is to have a simpler, more flexible life, not fill up my brain with facts. I'm sure it's a cool museum, but there's no inherent virtue in adding another random place to my collection of inaccessible memories.

Second, "should" is not the same as "want to." When I took that mental step back, I realized I'd rather go back to the campground and sit under my awning and think about the book I'm writing.

So I did.

Alas, nasty little stinging flies were chewing on my legs, so I didn't last outside for long. It lacks romance to admit that I retreated inside and hung out in the air-conditioning for the rest of the day, but that's what I did.

If I was camping — say on my one-week summer vacation from an office job, due back at work on Monday — I'd feel guilty for my wasted day. I could have been outside. I could have been kayaking. I could have been exploring the battlefields of Gettysburg, soaking in the history and tragedy of my location.

But living in a camper is not the same as camping, and it wasn't a wasted day.

In fact, today I think I will do the same thing. At the moment I'm sitting outside, listening to the noise of the bugs — so incredibly loud, beyond chorus levels and into rock symphonies — and watching the occasional wildlife. I've seen a chipmunk, squirrels and birds.

I heard a big splash in the water, which gave me an instant surge of adrenaline before I remembered that murky water + splash doesn't equal alligator in Pennsylvania. No idea what the splash was, but probably a fish, since I didn't see a bird. The flies are biting but not as badly as they were yesterday when it was hotter and I was sweatier.

Yesterday, I was joking with Tim over text about facing the challenge of the grocery store. The thing is, going to the grocery store did feel like a challenge. I had to pack up *Serenity*, unhook her from the electric and water, dump her tanks at the "sanitation station," navigate unfamiliar roads, start the generator to run the AC to keep the dogs cool, check on my alert system for a temperature reading inside the van. Even park more carefully than I did — I need to remember that *Serenity* is tall, because I again scraped her roof along trees, alas.

But it was exciting. And it was fun.

And I realized that I'm accomplishing (almost) exactly what I was vaguely, incoherently, hoping to accomplish. I've turned my life into an adventure, where even the small challenges, like going to the grocery store, require an eyes-wide-open approach, an appreciation of where I am and exactly what I'm doing. My heart is beating. It's a wonderful feeling.

It'll be even better when I'm also writing again. And that is going to happen. Maybe even today.

AUGUST 15, 2016 - GETTYSBURG, PENNSYLVANIA

I suffer from the relatively common ailment of mean brain. Not mean to other people, but mean to myself. It's something I've worked on for a long time, but I still have flare-ups.

Maybe it's like an allergic reaction? My hyperactive immune system thinks half the common substances on the planet are dire threats and stimulates misery in response. When my mean brain gets triggered, it stimulates misery, too. Maybe it's some kind of protective mechanism, but it's not a good one.

Sunday morning, it started whispering. I'll spare myself writing out the details — it's not like it's going to be good for me to spend more time in those thoughts — but the words "homeless" and "failure" were pretty loud.

Fortunately, I was in a good place to see those thoughts for what they were. Just words. Just labels.

Earlier I'd been sitting in my chair, watching the water and the trees and a chirpy little sparrow. The sparrow was adorable, totally charming in that tiny bird way. It kept a fearless eye on the dogs, but it was much more interested in whatever it was finding in the dirt.

It flew away and I thought, "What a miracle birds are."

And then one of the nasty biting bugs landed on my leg and I thought, "Hmm, I don't ever think about bugs being a miracle. But they can fly, too."

I waved the bug off and went inside to find some food. The campground was first-come, first-served, and I was reluctant to go get groceries while the weekend people were coming in. My spot was a mix of sun and shade, right on the water. It was also flat, with no major ruts or big muddy spots.

In other words, I was afraid to leave it for fear I'd lose it.

My food supply was running low but I made a salad from the dregs of the fridge. Before I ate, I took a picture, because it was pretty. As I sat down to eat, I was thinking about reality and how we shape it with our words.

Here's a reality: my nectarine was bruised. My cucumber was tasteless, no flavor at all. The radishes were getting squishy. The carrots seemed old the instant I opened the bag, slightly bitter and drying out. The salad greens are a week old, and heavy on some grassy thing I'm not nuts about.

Here's another reality: my egg was perfectly cooked and delicious. Still warm, it peeled easily and the yolk was exactly right. I made a fantastic dressing with mayo, olive oil, lemon juice and powdered ginger. It made the cucumbers delicious, the carrots tolerable, couldn't help the radishes, was interesting on the nectarine, and was amazing on the egg and the greens. I ate every last bite, even the grassy stuff.

And maybe those thoughts about reality and how we shape it were the trigger for me being mean to myself, but before I could do more than take two or three nasty swipes at my choices and my character, I caught sight of a fungus growing out of the picnic table where I was eating.

Ick. Gross. And yet, it was such a bright color, almost like a California poppy. And the curves of the stalks were like petals on a flower.

It was beautiful in the sunlight.

When my mean brain triggers, my eyes stop seeing the beauty around me. And in me, too.

They start labeling: bugs, fungus, homeless.

It is a reality that I have moments when I feel homeless, not adventurous. Three weeks ago, I had a perfect last day in my house, and the memory is bittersweet right now. I miss my pool. I miss my shower. I desperately miss my high-speed, always-on Internet connection.

And it's painful to be homesick for a home that you never get to go back to.

But my mean brain is not running this show. It's also a reality that I feel incredibly lucky. My salad was no different, no better than any salad I could have had a month ago at any time, but I appreciated it more.

A shift of the kaleidoscope wheel and the pieces are the same but the picture is changed.

AUGUST 18, 2016 - GETTYSBURG, PENNSYLVANIA

It rained last night, gloriously heavy, so that the pounding of drops on the roof of *Serenity* was like living inside a maraca. I wasn't being shaken, but the sound was that fast, heavy rattle. It was lovely.

But I'd decided when last I looked at the sky that the overcast white wasn't gray enough to bring real rain, so I left my chair and my towel and my purple-striped Mexican blanket outside.

They are well beyond damp.

I don't want them inside *Serenity*.

Honestly, I don't even want to touch the blanket. I put it down for the dogs because the ground here is hard gravel and dirt, with some puddles of mud, and I didn't want them — Zelda especially — to choose the mud puddles as the comfiest place to get cozy. Zelda would.

Bartleby also likes to roll in the dirt, but not with the same abandon. He's not a huge fan of baths and he's much more sensitive about the possibility of scolding. Zelda likes baths and she's seldom been scolded, so she luxuriates in the dirt, then comes in and goes straight to the tub without waiting to be ordered there.

With no tub, I don't know what she'd do, but tracking mud on my bed has never bothered her, so I'm pretty sure it would involve me needing to do laundry. I guess I'm going to have to do that anyway.

Dirt in general is turning out to be an unexpectedly challenging aspect of living in a camper. Campgrounds are dirty and dogs track in dirt and living partially outside and otherwise in a very small space means that there is a lot of dirt. I'm not a dirt-phobe, but I'm finding it harder to tolerate than I anticipated. Generally speaking when I go camping and things get dirty, I think, "I'll clean it when I get home."

Except this is home.

Yesterday the radio hosts on a show I was listening to were debating how many times one should use a towel before washing it. There was an actual, honest-to-goodness argument for once. Dry yourself with a towel one time and then wash it.

Um, no. I brought five standard towels with me and I've jettisoned two of them to take back the storage space they were using. I brought four or five dish towels with me, and that turns out to be not nearly enough.

Drying dishes, wiping spills, cleaning hands after cooking, drying hands, wiping off dogs' feet and bellies after coming in from a walk... at that point, the towel goes in the laundry bag and before I know it, I'm out of towels, and things are still getting dirty.

AUGUST 19, 2016 - WYOMING, PENNSYLVANIA

I walked Zelda this morning into a scene of stunning beauty. The full moon was still up, in a sky that had wisps of sunrise clouds, a subtle pink and twilight purple, in an otherwise overcast white. Mist was rising off deep dark rippling green water, and in the distance, the hills rolled. An artist could have drawn the classic three intersecting lines that anyone would recognize as hills in the distance and it would have been those exact three hills.

It wasn't bright, it wasn't showy, but it was so beautiful I had to hold my breath, as if breathing would shatter it.

I'm at Frances Slocum State Park. I came here because it was the closest camping spot to a cemetery I wanted to visit. Yeah, with the Grand Canyon and Mount Rushmore on my list of places to see, as well as the entire country of possibilities, my first destination was a graveyard.

But I've had my mom's ashes on my closet shelf for about four years now. She died five years ago and at the time I thought we'd do some family thing with her ashes after a suitable time. Long story short, eventually they wound up with me, and I've let them sit, not knowing what to do with them.

Frances Slocum State Park

Her last remains.

Except they aren't her last remains. I am what remains of her. R is what remains of her. The scrapbooks she created, those are her remains. My sister, my brother, their kids, our memories... so much remains of her.

And these ashes, they're not important, not really. But I did want to dispose of them respectfully. Even, I guess, lovingly. If there is any possibility that my mom's spirit is connected to the pile of gray dust that was her body, I wanted her to be happy with what happened to that dust.

That brings me to the cemetery. My great-grandmother is buried there, and I thought it would be nice to scatter a few of my mom's ashes on her grave. She loved her grandmother and treasured her memories of visiting her grandmother's farm when she was little. I wish I had any idea where the farm was, because that would have been perfect (barring the extreme discomfort of asking someone if they'd mind if you scattered ashes on their property and/or the likelihood that it's a housing development now), but the cemetery was the best I could do.

It was surreal.

I wandered through the gravestones looking for the right one — Myrtle Smith, with Paul Smith next to her — and instead finding, with vague shocks of recognition, everyone else.

My grandfather's parents. My grandfather's sister. My other great-grandparents. My great-great grandparents. Plenty of strangers' names, of course, but down every line, another Smith, Rozelle, Lewis, Labar, and Hahn.

It was eerie and charming and sort of heart-wrenching. I looked at what I thought was my great-grandparents' gravestone — Grover Cleveland and Jessie Labar — and knew almost nothing about them. I recognized their names but that was it.

In the end, I found the right grave and sprinkled a handful of my mom's ashes there. I didn't anticipate how emotional I would feel about it, how much it would bring my grief back to me and how sharp that pain would be.

The dead always outnumber the living in a cemetery, but being alone there, surrounded by my forgotten relatives, was hard.

Fortunately, this park is beautiful. The campsites are shaded, with screens of trees separating one site from the next. It's been rainy and muddy, but peaceful. (With the minor exception of my poor neighbors not having much success handling their whiny kids. The dad's exasperated, "What am I supposed to DO with her?" had me wincing in sympathy.)

AUGUST 25, 2016 - SOMEWHERE IN NEW YORK

When I was researching RVs, I read comments from several people that the Travato beds were as comfortable as their beds at home.

I know now the appropriate response to that should be, "Something is drastically wrong with your bed at home. You need to get yourself a new mattress."

The bed, as I'm referring to it, is actually two twin beds, with a low table set between them that supports two cushions, making an oddly-shaped, full-sized bed. Oddly shaped, because the two cushions don't add up to a twin-size length, so the top of the bed has a gap in the middle.

Before I got *Serenity*, I figured I'd just use my usual sheets and leave the bed set up all the time. I knew the first time I tried to make it that that would never work. If you've ever tried to make a bed in a corner, with walls on two sides, you know the experience, except this was trying to make a bed with multiple walled corners and a fitted sheet that didn't fit right.

I also realized that leaving the double bed up all the time made my space a lot less livable, since I had to crawl across it to reach my clothes and the bathroom and the switches to turn on the water or propane.

Initially I thought I could leave the beds made as twin beds — with both fitted sheets and flat sheets — and then put my queen-size fitted sheet on top when I set up the middle part of the bed at night. Didn't work. The four extra layers of fabric were enough that the cushions were hard to squeeze into place and prone to bumping up, making lumps in the bed.

I then wound up using two flat queen-size sheets, one as a bottom sheet, one as a top. But they worked their way loose because I'm a restless sleeper, making me an even more restless sleeper as my bed got uncomfortable and lumpy.

Yeah, I'm being very princess-and-the-pea about my sleeping arrangements.

I finally found a solution that mostly worked. I covered both twin beds with a fitted twin-sheet, and when I set up the middle, I covered the cushions with a flat twin sheet, edges tucked under. The bed was flat and neat and not lumpy. It's not perfect, but it's getting closer.

I've been living in Serenity for a month today. It doesn't feel like it. I'm still in a constant process of tweaking my space, searching for better solutions for storage and cooking and sleeping, even bathing. But it's been a good month: no disasters, no scares, no major downswings.

I don't feel comfortable yet — I'm still worried when I set up that I'll do something wrong and anxious when I'm trying to park.

And it's been so hot that the dogs have been a constant concern, which wasn't something I anticipated. The scope of what I imagine myself doing has narrowed drastically, because I can't leave the dogs, so no casual stops at restaurants or wandering around museums. That said, the dogs have been pretty good overall and they're adjusting.

And so am I. One month in, and I still feel lucky. My tiny house is indeed very tiny, but it's working.

AUGUST 29, 2016 - SOMEWHERE IN VERMONT

Vermont is exactly the way I imagined it would be. Well, summer time in Vermont. I also imagine that it's cold and gray and wintery and snowy, and it is none of those things. But it is green and peaceful and beautiful, with long stretches of empty roads and farms around every corner.

My first night I stayed at a Harvest Hosts site, a farm in New Haven, Vermont, right outside of Middlebury. I read a book while sitting under a tree, with corn fields before me and fields spreading out on all sides. I ate heirloom tomatoes and exotic cucumber with cheddar cheese, walked the dogs along a gritty white gravel road, and when I went to sleep — early! — I could see hundreds of stars from the window next to my bed.

Harvest Hosts is a membership site that lets you camp at farms,
wineries, museum, golf courses, and similar places.

In the morning, I took the craziest road, Route 17. A sign said something like "not advised for trucks in bad weather." The weather was fine, but the road was terrifying and entertaining in equal parts. Curvy, steep, and majorly bumpy. Things were crashing around in the back of the camper — the entire contents of the medicine cabinet spilled onto the floor — but the views and scenery were incredible.

My cousin C called while I was on the road, so when I saw a place to park, I pulled over to call her back. I decided to eat lunch there and my random, by-the-side-of-the-road parking lot turned out to be an access point to a river. Or maybe it was a creek?

I took the dogs down a flight of wooden stairs to a rocky beach where we sat and ate melon and prosciutto, then went wading. Even B tried the water, although that might have been because he knew I still had prosciutto. It was hot, probably in the low 80s, with the sun beating down, and the water — at wading level anyway — was pleasantly cool.

43

SEPTEMBER 2, 2016 - ONION RIVER CAMPGROUND, PLAINFIELD, VERMONT

For the past couple of days I've had no internet. Not slow internet, not bad internet. None, zip, nada.

Not even a phone connection.

It was sort of glorious.

Today didn't start out that way, though. This morning, I walked Z up to a high field and spent too much of the walk trying to get a cell phone connection, trying to check my email, annoyed at the bugs.

I tried to appreciate the subtle beauties of a gray day, the quiet colors of the late summer wildflowers, more subdued than spring flowers, but still shades of purple and gold and amber. I tried to find the forest lovely in its dark depths.

But you know what? I didn't. Not much, anyway.

Mostly I tried to find a connection and shooed off bugs and got annoyed at Zelda for continually getting her leash tangled in weeds. And when I finally decided that the bugs outweighed the merits of a one-bar internet connection that wasn't successfully managing to pick up my email anyway, I headed back down following a path that disappeared. We wound up shoving our way through tall, tall weeds, getting tangled up with burrs and nasty sticky plants, Z's leash tangling on every other strong stem, and me worrying steadily about ticks.

I kept trying to tell myself that it was an adventure. But it was damp and chilly — my jeans were soaked through from the knees down by the time I made it out of the field — and it mostly just felt annoying.

On the other hand, when we got back to *Serenity* and I dried us off and searched, I found no ticks. So hey, there's a blessing in disguise. Still, when a lack of ticks is the good news, you're definitely setting the bar low.

SEPTEMBER 5, 2016 - MONTPELIER, VERMONT

My cousin, C, knows half the people in Montpelier. Maybe more. We went out to dinner on Saturday night and she knew the people behind us in line. And then the guy sitting next to us at the bar. And then the guy who took his place, and the people on the other side of us, and the people on the other side of them.

Yesterday we went to Blueberry Lake, about an hour away from where she lives, and she ran into one person that she knew from college, another that she'd worked with, a third that she'd met once via a mutual friend.

It makes Vermont feel like a very small, very friendly place.

We've had an idyllic weekend. I met up with her on Friday night, after a frustrating day. (Note to self: more flexibility when it comes to meeting goals like finding decent internet and propane would go a long way to a happier life.)

We had crepes at a restaurant called The Skinny Pancake, then wandered around Montpelier. It's a great little city — cute shops, cafes, interesting restaurants. Multiple bookstores! That might be a sign of the long winters, but still, any town that can keep two independent bookstores thriving has a lot going for it. They had an art walk going on, with artists showing their work at local cafes so we checked out some interesting photography while we wandered and C said hello to every other person.

On Saturday, we went to the farmer's market which was a television stereotype, with vegetables, meats, cheeses, jams and pickles, interesting cooked food, some crafts, some music, plenty of people and dogs. If Stars Hollow from *The Gilmore Girls* had a farmer's market, it would look a lot like the Montpelier version.

Zelda and Bartleby came with me and were well-behaved and much admired. B loves this traveling business. People want to pet him and he soaks it up like a sponge.

In the afternoon, we took my inflatable kayak to a nearby lake for its first trial. The weather was exactly right for it — bright and clear, the water cool but not freezing. Zelda wore her doggie life jacket, which mystified her, but which worked exactly as advertised. When she went in the water (by her choice), she swam back to the kayak and I pulled her in using the handle on the life vest. It was perfect.

She seemed somewhat confused by the boat business, but after C and I finally figured it out (we were facing backwards, initially, which didn't work too well), she settled into the prow of the boat and took a nap while we paddled.

Bartleby however, was a total pest: he cried, he whined, he stressed, and then sometimes he wagged his tail, and eventually he slept a little, but he never seemed to enjoy it. He will not be going kayaking again.

I feel like I have so much more to write about — meeting up with relatives in Warren, our hike to Blueberry Lake, hanging out at a log cabin — but it's already after 11 and C and I are taking the dogs for a walk and then going kayaking again before barbecuing this evening — and so life is winning out over writing.

But while I was sitting on C's porch this morning, in her comfortable Adirondack chairs with cushions, surrounded by flowers, hummingbirds zooming by, eating blueberry pancakes and spicy scrambled eggs with sausage, I told her that the only problem with my travel plans is that there doesn't feel like enough time, not nearly enough to do all the things I want to do.

I want to stay longer, to see the leaves change color, to be here when the air gets crisp, and to savor the last days of sunshine. But tomorrow I head east. Maybe even by evening, I will be seeing the ocean, feeling sand underfoot and smelling salt. And even though more Vermont would be wonderful, I'm excited to watch my dogs run on the beach.

SEPTEMBER 8, 2016 - RECOMPENCE CAMPGROUND, FREEPORT, MAINE

On Tuesday, as I set off from Vermont, I thought, "I have the grays."

Not the blues, which would be too deep, too sad, too close to the core, but just the grays. And not even a dark gray, just a little translucent pearly gray.

But it was hard leaving Vermont, both figuratively in the sense that I was sorry to say good-bye and literally, because I had errands to run before I did and none of them worked out easily.

C took me to a great grocery store when we were short on time, so the first thing on my agenda was to go back and stock up on food. But around and around in circles I went. I thought I knew right where it was but I couldn't find it, and I just kept going in circles. Eventually I gave up.

The whole day felt like that. My propane tank read at $1/4$ full and I didn't want to chance running out if the weather got colder, so I wanted to fill it. Three stops for propane before the end of the day and all I accomplished was to learn that apparently the propane tank is hard to fill.

I'd run out of dog food a few days earlier and bought a fancy new kind at the great grocery store, but the dogs hated it. Even B wouldn't eat it after the first time and he eats anything. Z seemed perfectly willing to starve herself rather than touch her food and B seemed lethargic and unhappy. He didn't even want kibble. So I wanted the right dog food for them, one they were used to.

At one point, I passed a sign for PetSmart and I was so happy I actually thanked God for helping me find dog food. Unfortunately, the PetSmart was coming soon, not currently open.

By the time I got to the campground in Maine — with dog food, without propane, and with some not-very-well-chosen groceries, I was tired and cranky and didn't even want to explore. I fed the dogs and ate some of the not-very-good stew I'd made over the weekend and went to bed.

I'm discovering that it's hard to do anything by impulse while living in *Serenity*. Maybe that's good news? But playing it by ear or planning to go someplace on the spur of the moment just doesn't work.

Before I can drive somewhere, I have to pack up. Everything has to get stowed: dishes, the coffeemaker, electronics, the dogs' tie-out lines, the outside rug, the chair, the curtains, the power line, the water hose.

All the cabinets' locks have to be checked. The fridge lock, the medicine cabinet, the bathroom doors, all checked. The seats in the proper position, the window covers stowed, the rearview mirror repositioned.

It's not a trivial process.

I'm getting faster at it, I think. On Tuesday, I was ready to go by 8 AM when my cousin left for work. But I can't just decide to make a quick run to a restaurant for some seafood. There's no such thing as a quick run anywhere.

And that's okay, I think. My aunt, on Sunday, said to me that it sounded like I was living intentionally. I hadn't thought about it in that way before, but it resonated.

Yes, I'm trying to live intentionally.

And my intentions today are to appreciate my dogs, both of whom happily gobbled down their dog food this morning; to appreciate the coziness of my home; to maybe make myself many cups of tea; and to hopefully write some good words.

If all I ever see of Maine are the green trees around this campsite, that's okay.

SEPTEMBER 22, 2016 - SOMEWHERE IN MAINE

It's strange how often I think, "When I get home."

Example: I think I should cut my hair. Long hair is always a pain, but even more so when water is limited. While washing it, I've managed to overflow the gray tank, which means water around my ankles in the bathroom until I can get to a dump station. Short hair would rinse more quickly. So I think, "When I get home, I should cut my hair."

But this is home.

Wherever I am is home. For some things — doctor, dentist — it makes sense to stick with the people I know in Florida, but hair cuts, vet appointments, buying birthday presents for relatives, looking for a rug for the door area, picking up some better twin sheets — these are all things that can be done wherever I am.

And yet I think, "When I am home..."

I wonder how long it will take for that to wear off or if it ever will?

This morning, a flock of wild turkeys wandered through the campground. B was enraged, barking and growling and choking himself on the end of his tie-out cord in his determination to kill them all. Also kind of ridiculous, since the turkeys outnumbered and outweighed him.

He did scare them off, though, to my regret. I would have liked to watch them for a while. They had that elegant bird stalk, long necks bobbing as long legs delicately picked their way along the gravel path. Not attractive birds, but surprisingly graceful. Much, much skinnier than your average Thanksgiving bird.

And I'm guessing that they were wild turkeys, because that's the only slot in my head for birds of that size, that color, that shape, living in Maine.

SEPTEMBER 30, 2016 - SOMEWHERE IN WEST VIRGINIA

I'm having my first parking lot overnight.

To be honest, it's scary. I don't want it to be. I want it to be something that I take for granted, just an occasional free night of camping in an oasis of asphalt.

And this parking lot is really quite nice. It's an art center in West Virginia, and even though I didn't ask anyone if I could park here, I'm fairly sure from online reviews that it's allowed.

But it's raining, so the ground is wet and the windows are wet and everything is black and reflective and kaleidoscope-ish. The rivulets of water running down the windows make it feel like I'm living inside a Jackson Pollack painting.

R told me to put the curtains up and the blinds down and make myself a cozy little nest and I ought to follow his advice. I could then pretend I'm parked in a driveway, were it not for the highway noise. Maybe I could pretend the highway noise was the ocean.

So, yes, West Virginia. I'm having, in general, a surreal West Virginia experience. This afternoon a Monarch butterfly smashed against my windshield and got stuck on the wiper blade. Ugh, it was awful.

For the next twenty minutes, its wings fluttered in the wind and I couldn't tell if it was alive or dying or dead. I finally managed to pull over at a spectacularly beautiful scenic overlook and get it off.

Dead, unfortunately.

But then there I was at a spectacularly beautiful scenic overlook which I certainly wouldn't have stopped at had it not been for the butterfly. I kept thinking about chaos theory and what change might exist in the world because a butterfly crashed into *Serenity*.

But it also felt like a bad omen. Not that I really believe in bad omens. And I do think it's unfair of me to consider the death of a Monarch butterfly a bad omen when at least a dozen uglier bugs die every time I drive on the highway and I don't even notice, much less mourn their deaths.

Unfair or not, though, there it was: I continued on my path with my mood noticeably darkened.

Until, that is, I was crossing over a bridge and I saw a rainbow in my rearview mirror. A serious rainbow, all the colors, down so low — presumably because I was up so high in the mountains — that it felt like it was practically within touching distance. It's impossible to think that bad things are coming your way when you're looking at a rainbow.

Or at least it's a sign that if bad things are on their way, beautiful things will follow.

4

HOME SWEET HOME

OCTOBER 3, 2016 - SANFORD, FLORIDA

In the past ten weeks, I've camped in 22 different places.

- One state park
- One Harvest Hosts farm
- One parking lot
- One KOA
- Two independent campgrounds
- Four Passport America campgrounds
- Five Thousand Trails campgrounds
- Seven driveways

I loved the state park. If it had come later in my journey, I would have loved it even more because I would have realized how incredibly nice it was.

The Harvest Hosts farm was amazing, one of the best days, best experiences, of my first ten weeks.

The parking lot was interesting. As parking lots go, it was nice, but I suspect camping in parking lots is not going to be a huge factor in my life. I have never felt more Woman Traveling Alone than when I was awake at 3AM with street lights shining in my windows. I'm not sure I can relax enough to start enjoying your average Walmart parking lot anytime soon.

The independent campgrounds — from KOA (pricey) to Thousand Trails (free – $3/night) — were a mixed bag. The Onion River Campground in Vermont was so peaceful, such a pleasant place. But the Thousand Trails in upstate NY was the only place in my journey that I've been eager to leave behind. (My RV dealer included a Thousand Trails membership in my purchase price, which is why they're effectively free for me and why I stayed at so many of them.)

The seven driveways have been by far my favorite places to stay. I didn't expect that at all. I thought driveways would be uncomfortable, occasional places. But *Serenity* has enough solar power that unless I need air-conditioning to keep the dogs comfortable, it's easy to camp in a driveway.

Also reasonably private, usually quiet, and cozy. And sociable. I really didn't expect how sociable moving into a camper would be. I figured I'd be very isolated — plenty of time to do lots of writing — but not so much.

Today I'm in Christina's driveway. She gave me a key to her house and told me I should count her driveway as home base while I'm in central Florida. It made me tear up.

It's not that I need a key, although it's nice that I can take a shower without needing to wake anyone up. But it was a welcome mat, an invitation to stay for whatever time I need to stay.

I have these moments of feeling homeless, of feeling scared that there's no place to go back to, no place to be solid in the world. I'm floating, untethered, Mary Poppins-like drifting where the wind blows.

Sometimes I love that.

Sometimes, not so much.

I'm not going to move into Christina's driveway for a long stay anytime soon — I've got lots of places to go — but it feels like safety to know the option is there.

ON FINDING PLACES TO STAY

There are a ton of apps for campground research, but the two I mainly use are AllStays and Campendium. AllStays, because the interface makes it easy to see the type of campground, e.g. state park, county park, Army Corps of Engineers, and so on; and Campendium because, in my opinion, it has the nicest interface and the most helpful campground reviews of the apps I've tried.

OCTOBER 6, 2016 - SUWANEE RIVER STATE PARK, FLORIDA

I had plans for today.

In fact, most of my actions of the past two weeks have revolved around my plans for the next few days. Instead of drifting north, I rushed south, hurrying back to Florida. I was scheduled to help my friend Lynda with her table at the Orlando Indie Bookfest. We should be getting pedicures together today, and then dressing up for the author dinner.

Sadly, it is not to be. Hurricane Matthew is going to bash the east coast of Florida in less than 24 hours, hopefully not as hard as they're predicting at the moment, but definitely hard enough that people living in camper vans need to run for safer ground.

I had a brief conversation with my dad about places in central Florida where the van might be safe, and if it was just me and *Serenity*, I might have taken my chances. But Zelda and Bartleby need safety, too. That made it an easy decision, so yesterday morning I headed north and west. When I was sure I was out of the hurricane's path, I found a campground, the Suwannee River State Park.

It's typical northern Florida forest, lots of scrub pines and spiky palmettos on sandy ground covered with pine needles and leaves. Z and I had a good hike this morning, passing by the old sawmill equipment, wandering until we saw the springs gushing into the river. It was so profuse, it was like a mini waterfall, but you can only see the springs when the river is low. When it's high, they turn into a bubble in the water and when it's really high, the river water starts flowing into the springs instead. I think I'm mostly out of range of the hurricane, but it's predicted to rain for the next couple days, so it'll be interesting to see how the river changes, if it does.

I didn't expect to be here, I didn't plan to be here, but this is one of the most pleasant campgrounds I've visited. Quiet, with spacious sites and a serene peacefulness.

R would tell me that it's not irony that my unexpected destination is delightful, just a nice coincidence, but I'm not so sure.

OCTOBER 13, 2016 - VERO BEACH, FLORIDA

I'm attempting to bore myself into writing. It might be working, but if so, it's going slowly. Maybe by Monday I'll have made some progress.

I'm staying at the same campground for ten whole days. And not a beautiful or fun or inspiring campground — a parking lot campground. When I first got here, I thought it was creepy as hell. I wasn't sure I was going to stay even for two days, much less ten.

The next day, I realized the creepiness — a general impression of a ramshackle, disheveled ghost town — was the result of the hurricane. It's been fun to watch them clean it up, one stretch after another going from debris-strewn to neat and tidy.

Plus, they have a dog park, which is a huge fenced field. I've been working on improving the dogs' stays and recalls, and a big space gives them a chance to practice. Alas, status quo remains: Zelda's a rocket scientist and Bartleby doesn't have a clue.

I tell Zelda to stay and she sits and trembles and waits as I get farther and farther away, until finally I turn and point at the ground and she barrels toward me at joyous hyper speed, her ears trailing behind her, as if she actually thought I might leave her behind.

Bartleby, on the other hand, bounces along two steps after me no matter what I say or do. But hey, eight more days in this park gives us a lot of time to practice.

My sister tells me I write about Z a lot and rarely about B. I think that's because B doesn't usually come on our long walks — Z needs plenty of exercise, but B can't walk that far. But just in case she's not the only one who wants to know how they're doing with the traveling lifestyle:

B loves it madly. He is more energetic, more rambunctious, happier and bouncier than he has ever been. He gets adored in campgrounds. All small children instinctively gravitate to him and he takes their attention and sticky hands as his due. He has entirely stopped hiding under furniture and in closets, perhaps partially because there aren't a lot of places to hide in *Serenity*, but he doesn't even try anymore. Instead, he cuddles up next to me and suggests I pet him.

He's looking great, too. People have commented that he's lost weight and he might have, but he also just seems sleeker and shinier and healthier. And happier. In Massachusetts, I confidently said, "Bartleby doesn't play," just as he tore across the room and grabbed a tennis ball ahead of Zelda before returning it to my uncle, tail wagging.

Z, on the other hand... I think she likes parts of it. She likes our morning walks. She likes exploring new places, sniffing new smells. But it also seems to stress her out more than I expected. She's gotten even pickier about her food, often rejecting her kibble entirely.

She's also being clingy. She's always been a very attached dog — the feeling is mutual, I'm very attached to her, too — but her level of worry that I might disappear seems to have increased. As long as she's touching me, she's calm, but she seems more high-strung.

Although now that I'm analyzing this, she has adjusted to *Serenity* as home. She's fine about being left in *Serenity*. She's just not fine about being left in other people's houses, which I've had to do because it's been too hot to leave her in the van when I can't run the AC. Hmm, so I just need to go to colder climates to keep the dog happy. Works for me.

SARAH WYNDE

OCTOBER 24, 2016 - SOMEWHERE IN FLORIDA

On Friday, I left my campground in Vero Beach with some unexpected regret. I truly thought ten days of sitting still, all alone, would make me stir-crazy, but I was completely peacefully happy.

And the writing went incredibly well — it was writing like I haven't experienced since, I think, February 2014, which is an awfully specific date, but that was when Fen was spilling out of me like she was writing *A Lonely Magic* by herself.

Since I was on the road, though, I decided we should have an adventure. I headed for Captain Forster Hammock Preserve, a dog-friendly park that according to Bring Fido, an app for traveling with dogs, included a pleasant $^3/_4$ mile hike to a beach.

I got lost on the way and wound up driving on a dirt road for about forty minutes, through mud puddles galore, but eventually found the park and took the dogs for a walk.

Not, however, a $^3/_4$ mile hike to the beach.

The post-hurricane mud puddles had turned the trails into slip-and-slides, as well as creating perfect breeding grounds for a mosquito world domination plan. When B sat down and refused to go any farther — I think we were getting close to the beach, but I couldn't say for sure — I decided to take his opinion as law.

As we headed back inland, I was thinking about the rest of my plans for the day and wishing I could write. As I was thinking that, I drove past a... well, sort of a park, I guess?

It was a parking lot. With one pavilion and one picnic table and plenty of room for cars. But it was right by the water. Impulsively, I pulled into it and parked, parallel to the water. I got out my computer, and for the next three hours, I wrote to the sound of ocean waves, the smell of sea, with a cool breeze coming in through the open windows. It was paradise.

One of the best things about *Serenity* are her windows. A lot of RVs, especially the smaller ones, feel closed up. The wall space is used for storage and appliances and it feels like you're sitting inside a box.

But the Travato 59K has long windows running along the twin

beds. In fact, the K basically has windows everywhere it's possible to put a window. Even the bathroom has windows on the doors.

When I was looking at it, I liked it because of the light it let in. I thought living in a box would likely be easier if it was a well-lit box. But now that I've lived in her for a while, I love it because of the views.

I love lying in the bed at night, turning my head two inches to the left to see the night sky. And I love working in my office (the same bed, sitting propped against the window) and looking up from the computer to see trees and leaves and sometimes — when I'm smart enough to stop at a parking lot by the water — an incredibly blue ocean.

Parked next to the water.

OCTOBER 31, 2016 - ORLANDO, FLORIDA

Last Monday, I was waiting for a friend to get home, so I could get into her house and start cooking dinner. It was late —around 7:30 — and I was starving, so while I waited I made side salads. On a base of mixed greens, I added red onion, red pear, radish, and cucumber, topped with balsamic vinegar.

She still hadn't arrived and like I said, I was hungry, so I put together an appetizer plate, too: dates wrapped in prosciutto and some olives and crackers. When she got home, I got the salmon out of her fridge, topped it with some lemon preserves, and put it under her broiler. About fifteen minutes later, we were eating dinner.

On Saturday, I showed up at the same friend's house. We had plans, but we were both tired. Around six, we finally decided — well, I think I finally decided — that we should just eat at home. I had chicken thighs, so I sprinkled an herb mix (coriander, chili, cumin, parsley) over them, tossed in some dried apricots, and stuck them in the oven. While they baked, I made some brown rice, and salads of mixed greens, chopped dried apricot, pecans, avocado, radish, green onions and tomatoes.

While we were eating, E gave me the loveliest compliment on my cooking. I wish I remembered her exact words. It was something about simplicity. Actually, I think she first said that I was an incredible cook, and I pointed out that baked chicken thighs and salad are pretty much lowest common denominator. It's not even possible to ruin a salad and it would be tough to mess up baked chicken thighs.

And this wasn't a planned meal: I just pulled stuff out of my cabinets and fridge because we were being lazy. I guess, though, that was her point, because she said something along the lines of while she was sure I could cook intricate meals, it was my ability to make simplicity wonderful that she admired. Something like that. And it's funny that I can't remember the exact words, but I still feel the glow of pleasure they gave me.

When I got to her house that day, I was feeling stressed and over-tired and drawn back into a world of responsibility and worry. But we took the dogs for a long walk, then sat in her back yard and admired the trees and the birds. While I cooked dinner I felt an internal hum of satisfaction of being in a kitchen creating and while we ate, I was almost purring with the delight of delicious food. Good food when you're hungry and tired is so satisfying.

By the time I fell asleep in *Serenity* that night, I was calm and mellow and happy again.

I wish I could become someone who knows instinctively that what I need when I'm feeling off is outside time, exercise, healthy food, creation, and companionship. Because earlier on Saturday what I wanted was computer time and junk food and solitude. The healthy choices — the healing choices — aren't intuitive to me. Still, maybe each time I learn this lesson it sinks in a little more.

NOVEMBER 3, 2016 - ST. AUGUSTINE, FLORIDA

I'm staying at a state park. The Atlantic ocean and miles of sandy beach are easy walking distance away. But I haven't touched it and have only seen it once.

Traveling with dogs is totally worthwhile, but also more challenging than I expected. When I say "easy walking distance," I mean easy walking distance for Zelda and me, not for Bartleby. It would be a long, long walk for him and an even longer walk for me if I wound up carrying him.

But that's irrelevant because dogs aren't allowed on the beach. If I wanted to go to the beach, I'd have to leave both dogs behind in *Serenity*.

Want to know what else is not allowed? Leaving your dogs unaccompanied at your campsite. And actually, I'm sympathetic to that: the chance definitely exists that both dogs would bark miserably the whole time I was gone, if I wanted to leave them, which I don't.

So I'm at the beach, but not enjoying the beach.

Fortunately, I'm enjoying my campsite. It's peaceful and quiet, tucked back in a corner of a reasonably empty campground.

Two nights ago I was a little freaked out by its isolation as I listened to loud rustling in the bushes, but I finally dug out my flashlight and shone it out on the raccoons climbing the tree about ten feet away from my window.

I was then still a little freaked out — raccoons are big when they're so close and there were two of them — but hey, it wasn't a bear or a serial killer, so I did relax enough to go to sleep eventually.

I've had some great walks around the campground. A loop called the Ancient Dunes loop is supposedly a pleasant half hour walk, presumably for people who aren't being walked by a fast-paced Jack Russell terrier, but it's a fun up-and-down trek on a sandy path through the Florida forest. Lots of mosquitoes, of course, and they do love me, and a few too many spiders who built their webs across the path — sorry, spiders, for destroying all your hard work, and ick, ick, ick, spider webs on me — but it's so primeval that you can almost imagine yourself in the Jurassic.

NOVEMBER 18, 2016 - ORLANDO, FLORIDA

On Tuesday, my writing group friends reminded me that our monthly dinner would be Wednesday night. Unfortunately, I was at a campground about ninety minutes away. Lynda offered me her driveway — a nice long driveway, with plenty of room — but my instinctive response was, "No, I can't, I'm at this campground for another two days."

It took me a while to question myself. Why was I staying at the campground when I could be going out to dinner with friends?

Why did I feel locked in to a commitment that I had made to absolutely no one? The campground didn't care if I left early, and it was a Thousand Trails campground so it wasn't costing me much money. And even if it had been, the money was spent, one way or another, and it wouldn't cost me anything extra to go spend the night in L's driveway instead.

So Wednesday morning, I packed up and headed north. What a great decision. I had a fun day of writing with L, an excellent dinner with a terrific group of people, and many good conversations about writing.

At dinner A asked me what had surprised me about life in the camper. I don't think I said this then, although I might have, but one of the things that has surprised me is how uncomfortable I am with uncertainty. I like knowing where I'm going to be spending the night. I like having my calendar mapped out.

I want adventures and new places, but I'm much more prone to deciding where I'll be camping two weeks out and then sticking to that decision than I am just going where the wind takes me.

But I want to work on that. I think I need more days of going where the wind takes me. Being flexible, being willing to be spontaneous, being able to live with uncertainty, is part of living in the now.

I want to be able to embrace the uncertainty.

NOVEMBER 19, 2016 - LAKE LOUISA STATE PARK, FL

This morning's sunrise was supremely beautiful, beyond words. The water was still and clear, mist rising from it with enough of a breeze that the mist quickly drifted by, a fast-paced cloud. Behind it, through it, over it, the sun was slowly changing the colors of the sky. It was a pastel rainbow reflected in the water, so beautiful it was like being inside one of those scenic photographs that I skeptically think have probably been Photoshopped to death.

A noise from behind me was so loud and so weird that I thought some strange steampunk vehicle must be coming my way. It was a flock of tiny birds, shadows of black against the sky, spiraling up and away, and squeak, squeak, squeaking like wheels desperately in need of some oil.

A huge spider — seriously, huge — had built a perfect web at precisely the distance from the walkway where I could admire it without being completely freaked out by having a huge spider near me. One step forward and the web disappeared, one step backward and it did the same, but at exactly the right angle, right position, I could see the fine lines of silk against the backdrop of blue sky.

The water had lily pads, lots of them, but also water grass, and the water grass looked like it ought to be out of some movie with dinosaurs. I'm calling it grass because it was shaped like grass, flat stalks tapering to a point, but it was huge, probably at least four feet high, and thick as my arm, colored red and green, and when the sun finally rose high enough, golden as the sun hit it.

I should probably go take some pictures. But it's too late for the sunrise, and photographs, mine at least, never capture the real beauty of a scene. It would be missing the cool breeze, with air brisk enough that my nose got chilled. And the morning stillness that can encompass noisy birds, rustles in the brush, the occasional splash in the water, and yet still feel silent. And nothing about a photograph would ever convey the sense of awe I felt, the wonder.

Or, for that matter, the growl of my stomach and need to pee that finally motivated me to turn my back on the water and head home.

NOVEMBER 28, 2016 - TRIMBLE PARK, MOUNT DORA, FL

This morning's sunrise was so pure, with the sun sliding up the horizon, completely unencumbered by clouds. The sunset last night was amazing in a totally different way — lots of clouds, lots of layers, many shades of purple and red, going on for what felt like forever. And the sunrise yesterday morning was pretty nice, too. The night before, sunset, also spectacular. Sunrise that day, also lovely.

Sunset and sunrise are so ordinary. We all get them, every single day. They are the epitome of the everyday, in fact. And yet, in my current life, I spend so much time appreciating them.

It's something about being in new places all the time. Well, okay, also sunsets (and rises) over water are twice as spectacular as the ones without water. It's the reflection that does it, of course.

And when you're sitting on a bench next to a fire pit watching the sky while a giant, gawky bird with legs longer than its body goes flapping by, awing you with the miracle of flight, appreciation comes easier than when you're sitting in rush hour traffic, worried whether you're going to make it to the daycare before they start charging $10/minute.

Of course, the corollary to spending more time appreciating sunset and sunrise, water and birds, spider webs and flowers is that I also spend a lot more time wondering how I'm going to get my laundry done. Or whether the grocery store is going to have the right dog food. Or how close the nearest Banfield is when a dog has yet another ear infection.

It's like my life is simultaneously sort of ethereal and sublime and also really mired in the daily necessities of existence, much more so than when I lived in a house and the question was just, "Do I need to do laundry?" not "How am I going to get my laundry done?"

The line in the water is a bird, taking off.

On Saturday, I was walking the dogs with E. I was crossing the road when I glanced behind me and saw that she and Bartleby had paused. I was the one carrying the clean-up bags, so I paused, too, to see if I needed to go back. Z kept going, though, tugging me along, so I took a few steps forward.

Then I looked around and realized that I was standing on the double yellow lines, in the middle of the road, walking forward along them. It felt thrilling. There was no traffic coming, so it didn't feel dangerous. But the yellow lines beckoned the way ahead of me, like the yellow brick road in the *Wizard of Oz*.

I said to E, "I don't think I've ever walked on the yellow lines before. I'm not really a middle of the road kind of person. I'm a safely on the side of the road person. Or better yet, a sidewalk person. It's sort of weird."

She laughed at me and then her expression changed. I could see her go thoughtful before she said, "You know, I don't think I've ever walked along the yellow lines either." So then she joined me in the middle of the road, and we walked down the yellow lines until we reached the corner and another sidewalk. It was ridiculously fun, in the way adventures that aren't really adventurous can be.

ON VETS WHILE TRAVELING

Both my dogs had wellness plans at Banfield Pet Hospital, a chain located mostly inside PetSmarts. Their medical records were computerized, so when they needed care, any Banfield tech could access their medical histories. This was convenient, far more often than I would have liked.

DECEMBER 1, 2016 - TRIMBLE PARK, MOUNT DORA, FL

I built a campfire the other night, right before sunset. While the sun slid down into the water, which rippled with pink and purple and rose and gold reflected light, and the sky gradually grew dark, I watched the flames flicker and leap. Doesn't that sound lovely?

It would have been if I hadn't spent so much energy worrying about alligators. My campsite is right next to the water and the fire pit is about eight feet from the shoreline.

I don't know what my thing is about alligators. I mean, yes, the dogs are the perfect size to be alligator meals, and yes, alligators are actually much faster than they look when they're resting, and yes, they've got the whole dinosaur, primeval, lumpy reptile thing going on. But still, people don't often lose their pets to wandering 'gators.

Trimble Park is the campground closest to my dad's house, but also a beautiful place. It's only got 15 spaces, though, so can be hard to get reservations.

And while this park definitely has alligators in it — I'm fairly sure I saw an eye peering out of the water at me the other day and my neighbors claimed they've seen one clearly — the alligators are just as likely — more likely, actually! — to be small. Two foot long alligators, not ten foot long. Rodent-eaters, not dog-eaters.

In the darkness, though, the water felt much too close.

At one point, I thought I saw a shadow by the edge of the water. Not an alligator shadow, an animal shadow. Like a cat. I told myself I was imagining things, and then the shadow started moving. It was on the other side of the fire and it wandered by the edge of the water, a dark motion against darkness.

For a couple minutes, when I wasn't sure whether it was really there or not, I thought of fae and fantasy, creatures out of Patricia Brigg's novels or JK Rowling. Then it moved enough into the light that I was sure it was real and I decided it was probably a raccoon.

Yesterday my neighbors found a snake in their campsite. I think it was a garter snake, but the dad told the kids it was venomous, maybe just to make sure they stayed away from it. Why take chances, after all? Then when I was walking Zelda, we came upon a turtle in the road. It immediately stopped being a turtle and started being a dark green and yellow rock, head and feet drawn inside. Zelda was more curious about why I was stopping our walk to take a picture then she was about the turtle. I guess turtles don't smell as interesting to dogs as Spanish moss does. I also had to chase a lizard out of the kayak. I considered taking it kayaking with me, but decided it probably wouldn't enjoy the ride and if it fell in the water, I'd feel guilty.

This morning, while walking Z, I saw another critter in the woods. No idea what it was, except maybe a big armadillo? It was far enough away that I didn't get a good look, and moving quickly, but the silhouette looked wrong for every animal in my mental repository of Florida appropriate animals, including armadillo. Anteater and tapir were the shapes that came to mind.

So yes, animals. Reptiles. Great campground. I love all the little moments of excitement that random strange animals bring into my life.

DECEMBER 8, 2016 - SOMEWHERE IN FLORIDA

I know solitary confinement is torture, but part of me thinks I'd do just fine with it. I'd prefer it if it included my dogs and a loaded ebook reader and something to write with and on, preferably keyboard-oriented, of course, but even without all that, I think I'd be okay. I've never been one of those people who can't stand their own company and after almost twenty years of mostly working from home, I'm good at solitude.

Obviously, that doesn't stop me from getting lonely – everyone is lonely sometimes – but I didn't worry about loneliness being a problem in my traveling life. I considered it, but I thought I'd be fine. And I am.

Mostly.

But I'm discovering that loneliness is deeper, at least for me, when it comes with joy. When I'm having a bad day or something's gone wrong, I might want someone to vent to or even get help from — I spilled coffee this morning and it would have been nice if someone could have grabbed the computer while I was getting the dogs out of the way — but generally, the thought doesn't even occur to me. I grumble to myself or to the dogs, and I try to take my time with problems and if I really need help, well, that's what the phone is for. I don't usually feel lonely because something's gone wrong.

But when something's gone right, when I see an incredible sunrise or a mysterious animal or have a funny story I want to share (like the text I got from R in Canada, where he said, "It is a mark of how Floridian I am that when I first started seeing icicles I thought they were decorations," which makes me smile every time I think of it), that's when I notice how alone I am.

I'm still okay with it — it's not like I'm in solitary confinement, my solitude is not breaking my spirit or driving me insane — but those are the moments when I feel lonely.

DECEMBER 15, 2016 - SOMEWHERE IN FLORIDA

I saw an owl this morning.

It flew across the sky in the pre-dawn light, clearly a bird. Clearly a big bird. My brain had to process. What is that bird?

In Florida, the default on a big bird is vulture. That's what we've got the most of. But this bird didn't say vulture to me. The wings were wrong. The flight was so smooth, such a glide, so quiet. Eagle? No. Hawk? No. Falcon?

The bird settled on a tree branch and finally my brain — in my defense, it was early, before coffee — put together the flight, the time of day, the size of the bird, its silhouette on the tree branch, and the calls of Whoa-whoa-whoa-whooooo that I was hearing and said, "Owl."

Actually, it was more like my brain said, "Owl. Owl, owl, owl, owl, OWL!"

I've seen them in captivity and I've seen them in photographs and once or twice, I've seen one in the wild from a distance when someone pointed it out to me, but this was my first real close-up of a wild owl.

And then another one flew by, and the first one joined it and they tried a different tree. I tried to follow them, but they moved again, deeper into the fenced-off forest that surrounds the campground, and I resumed walking with Zelda. But my morning no longer felt prosaic and dusty, but a little bit magical.

Owls are cool.

DECEMBER 19, 2016 - BLUE SPRINGS STATE PARK, FL

I'm camping in Blue Springs State Park this week, famed as a home to manatees in winter time. I've visited this park before as a day visitor, more than once, so it's not new to me. But this morning while I was walking Zelda, I was imagining myself in a post-apoca-lyptic world. The kind where plague has taken all the people, not zombies.

I wasn't scared, it just felt incredibly empty. Every other time I've been here, there have been lots of people, but of course, that was never before dawn.

Then I spotted some manatees in the water and got much more cheerful, because probably if the human beings all died out, the manatees would have a much better chance of surviving.

The pros of the apocalypse.

Last night, it rained. My weather app — which honestly, seems fairly useless, except for the immediate weather — had been claiming rain for days, including an entire afternoon of lightning and thunder yesterday, but it didn't happen until 4:43 AM this morning.

I can be so precise about the time because I woke up and it had barely started, a little tap-tap-tap on the roof of *Serenity*, but as I lay there wondering what that noise was, it really started. It went very quickly from tapping to torrential, which sounds a lot like being inside a drum. Or maybe a heart beat. I haven't had nearly enough rain in *Serenity*, because I do enjoy it so. Last night, I could hear the difference in the sounds of the rain hitting the roof and the rain hitting the plastic vents over the fans. It was music, definitely.

Albeit slightly boring music after ten minutes or so. Plenty of rhythm, but a lack of harmony.

DECEMBER 22, 2016 - BLUE SPRINGS STATE PARK, FL

Yesterday I was walking Z in the very early morning. Pre-dawn, but not so pre-dawn that it was still dark. I'd taken her up a white sandy road that led past the dumpsters out of the campground. The road had a "No Vehicles" sign posted but no other signs, so I wasn't sure where it led, but since we were just walking for the sake of walking, it didn't matter to me.

It was incredibly lovely. The still of the early morning, nothing manmade in sight except for the road itself.

Just me and Z, alone in the world.

Then I saw a flash of dog, tall dog, just a glimpse of leg and tail, crossing the path a long way in front of us.

Dang it.

You never know with off-leash dogs — are they off-leash because their owners have trained them well or are they off-leash because their owners are terrible owners?

Jack Russell terriers are genetically incapable of backing down from a fight. If Zelda decides a dog is a threat to me, she'll get aggressive and its size won't deter her. Although she's never gotten aggressive with a dog smaller than her, only dogs bigger than her, so I guess size does deter her, just not in a fearful way. Still, I'm wary of bringing her near strange off-leash dogs that she might decide need to be taught a lesson.

I paused and the dog disappeared.

Zelda, on our beautiful, peaceful road at just about sunrise.

It looked like it disappeared into the brush, but that seemed unlikely, so I decided the road must have a path I couldn't see leading away. But since the dog and its owner were moving on, I stopped worrying.

I kept walking. It was chilly, at least by Florida standards, but I was enjoying the cool air and the brush of moisture in the fog. Then I saw the dog again.

Or dogs rather, because now there were three of them. Tall, skinny, and a matched set, all a gray brown with flags of white on their tails.

Someone had a pack of dogs.

A pack of dogs that they were letting run off leash.

In a state park.

In fact, in a wilderness area.

Yeah, I don't think so.

I stopped walking.

Two of the coyotes disappeared into the brush, but the third stood where it was and stared at me.

I stared back.

It wasn't really close, not so close that I felt immediately threatened. And I did, in fact, have a little mental debate of whether I wanted to keep going on the path that I had been so enjoying and trust my presence would scare them off.

Coyotes aren't known for attacking people.

But — my thought process continued — coyotes are known for attacking small animals and I'm walking with a small animal that I love very much and who would never back down from a fight, even if it was with an entire pack of coyotes.

Also, I'm not the biggest of human beings myself. I'm not short, but I don't think anyone would ever suggest that I could be threatening. Even to dogs. And these weren't small dogs, they were definitely long-legged and tall. And like I said, skinny, so maybe they were hungry.

Also out in daylight, and daylight plus night-time predators could definitely mean hungry predators.

So I took some careful steps backward, not letting my eyes off the watchful coyote, and then turned around and walked back to the campground, taking my beloved coyote breakfast with me.

DECEMBER 29, 2016 - SANFORD, FLORIDA

Night before last, my fan went crazy. I bet that's the kind of description that drives mechanics crazy, too, but believe me, it is an apt description.

When the craziness settled out, it was beeping. Beep. Five second pause. Beep. Five second pause. Beep.

Five seconds is just long enough that there was no way to turn the beep into background noise. No possible way to ignore the noise, convince myself that it was cicadas or an annoying bird, no way to fall asleep between beeps and not wake up for the next one.

Five seconds is maddening.

By 6AM, I was at my RV dealer (getting sent away by the security guard) and by 7:45AM, I was back at my RV dealer, plaintively begging for help. I didn't have an appointment, of course, and they don't take walk-ins, but they said they'd take a look and at least cut power to the fan and shut it up.

While I sat on a couch in their showroom, dogs beside me, desperately wishing for sleep, I catalogued *Serenity*'s problems.

There was the leaky air-conditioner that let so much water in the first night that the beds got soaked. The window that once opened wouldn't close. The screens that weren't properly placed in their tracks. The propane tank that wouldn't fill. The thermostat that didn't measure the temperature correctly. The sticky drawer latch that led to the facing of the drawer pulling off, exposing bare nails. The sink latch that jammed, had to be replaced, promptly broke again, and while I waited for my service appointment to get it fixed a second time, let the sink bounce around enough that the hinges on the sink broke, leaving the sink dangling half off the wall. The dead awning which fortunately died while closed.

And then, of course, the fan going crazy.

All that in the first six months of ownership.

I was filled with gloom and doom. After the air-conditioning and until the fan, none of the problems had been major livability issues, but what next?

And then I took a deep breath and began reframing.

The air-conditioner was fixed. I don't open the window that's hard to close. I got the screens into their tracks and yes, it was a pain, but they work fine now. The propane tank's sensor reset once the tank was empty and now I know to tell the guy filling it to go slowly. The thermostat was user error, albeit based on unclear instructions, but still, no longer a problem. The drawer had been repaired. The sink was scheduled for repair. The awning was scheduled for repair. The only real problem was the fan.

And I went to Vermont. I watched the sunrise over farm fields and mountains, and waded in a mountain stream with the dogs. I sat next to the ocean and wrote. I've seen owls and coyotes and manatees. I've visited relatives and friends, gotten to have real time with people that I hadn't seen in years. Ate chocolate cake with my dad and stepmom on Christmas Eve.

The service guy came back. He told me they'd pulled the fan out and ordered a new part for it, but wouldn't be able to get it fixed until the part came in, some time in the next couple of weeks, but that they'd stopped the noise. Oh, and that they'd fixed the sink and the awning. I hugged him.

I'm not excited about how many things have gone wrong with *Serenity* and I'm not looking forward to whatever goes wrong next. But the last thing I have to do in Florida now (depending on when the part for the fan comes in) is a vet appointment on the 10th of January, which means that in less than two weeks, I can head west.

Alabama, Louisiana, Mississippi, Texas — there are so many places I want to go, so much I want to see, so much I want to do.

5

HAPPINESS

I was near Sarasota this weekend, mostly so I could see R, with a side dollop of managing some paperwork with him. Honestly, if the paperwork hadn't existed, I would still probably have gone to Sarasota because one breakfast was not nearly enough after not having seen him for six months.

I got here late — I think it was my first arrival after dark, which I'd been cautioned against. It was sort of thrilling, doing a slow drive through the wilderness, the only light my headlights, then finding my campsite and getting myself situated.

It made me think about the dark, though.

I'd like to know when I learned to be afraid of the dark and how. It wasn't when I was little. I can remember loving being outside on winter nights when the sky was black and the stars were out.

When I visited my grandparents, my siblings and I slept in a furnished basement with no windows. We had a nightlight, because without it, the room was pitch-black, not even a sliver of light from under the door.

I loved it, though. It was fun to stumble around, thrilling to lose myself and not know where I was in the room anymore. I can't remember ever worrying about monsters, under the bed or anywhere.

Then I grew up. And of course I learned that the dark was dangerous, especially to women.

I resent that so much.

Z's stomach was unhappy so I wound up walking her twice. The night was beautiful. An evening breeze, moonlight and starlight, the smells of nature, somehow more intense in the dark.

I miss so much because I have to worry about my safety.

But do I have to? Is that worry a choice?

Every time I don't go for a walk in the dark, because the dark is scary and women aren't safe at night, I lose out. I'm being deprived of twilight and deep night, starry skies, crescent moons.

And really, why? Do I honestly think the average campground has criminals hovering around the corner, waiting for their opportunity to attack me? Vampires? Werewolves?

I think it's time to start walking Z in the evening, as well as the morning. A real walk for both of us, maybe not too late, but late enough that we get to appreciate the stars.

Oscar Scherer is gorgeous at sunrise. Actually, it's gorgeous all the time.

JANUARY 19, 2017 - MOUNT DORA, FLORIDA

I'm having so much fun playing with Roadtrippers.com. I haven't really planned out my previous adventures, except in terms of which family member or friend I was headed to visit next, with stays at Thousand Trails campgrounds or state parks between visits and errands.

But I decided I needed to map out my next few weeks while I had plentiful internet access, so I spent a big chunk of the past few days reading links and being alternately wistful about the things that don't make sense to do with two dogs in tow and excited about the ones that do.

In other words, no Mardi Gras, even though I'll probably be in the right area around the right time. But Dauphin Island might work out and it looks amazing.

I say "might" because I'm not making reservations. Not yet. *Serenity* is in for service again today and I'm... well, not doubtful, exactly. But I lack faith.

I'm not thrilled about getting so comfortable at the RV dealer's service facility that I bring my own coffee cup along to help myself to their coffee, and that the people who work there are becoming familiar. There are three women at the service counter and I have a favorite, the one whose line I prefer to get in. (The cheerful, helpful one, of course.) That's not a good sign. But fingers crossed, today might be the day I'm done for a while.

Serenity did get a nice upgrade this week. My dad and a family friend installed a shower curtain rail for me in the bathroom. I'm waiting for clips to actually hang the curtain, so I can't say for sure what it's going to be like, but I'm optimistic that this will make showering in the van seem like less of a project.

Previously, every shower required attaching the shower curtain to snaps along the ceiling and walls to protect the closet and drawers, and it was annoying.

Showering in the van isn't great anyway. It's fine for so-called Navy showers. Get wet, stop the water, soap up, turn the water back on, and rinse off. If I try to condition my hair, though, chances are I'll either run out of hot water or fill up the gray tank faster than is convenient. It's almost always easier and more comfortable to use a campground shower. But at least when I need to shower in the van, it won't be quite so much work now.

JANUARY 31, 2017 - DAUPHIN ISLAND, ALABAMA

A few days ago, while I was driving, I was trying to count the number of states I've visited. You'd think that would be easy. It's basically a yes, no question, after all.

Have I been to California? Yes, I have.

Have I been to Alaska? No, I haven't.

Nothing complicated about that, right?

But there are states I'm uncertain about.

Indiana? My brother went to college there, and I'm sure I visited him, so yes, although the details are lost to the mists of time.

New Hampshire? I've driven through it on the way to Maine more than once, but did I ever get out of the car?

Alabama used to be one of those. I knew I must have driven through it before — it's on the way from California to Florida when you're driving through the south — but I didn't remember anything about it.

Now I'll never forget it.

I'm staying on Dauphin Island, at the Dauphin Island Campground. The campground, well… isn't a state park. I'd love to understand why the independent campgrounds have so much more of a problem with litter. The first thing I did when I stepped out onto my campsite was pick up some receipts, a bottle cap, and a candy wrapper and throw them in the trash.

But steps away from *Serenity*'s door is a path into the bird sanctuary and down to the beach.

On our first morning here, Z and I were on the beach in time to see the sun rise. I saw a flash of black in the water, then another, then realized I was watching porpoises feeding. It was thrilling.

Every day I've roamed through more of the sanctuary, exploring different trails. The birds are incredible. It reminds me of the aviaries in Disney's *Animal Kingdom*, birds everywhere, flitting back and forth across the path in front of me, sitting in trees, standing or floating in the water, lined up on the rocks, swooping across the sky.

And the noises! Dozens of different sounds, tweets and chirps and trills and taps. It's like living inside a video game. Some of their calls sound like words to me — there's one that says, "Secrets, Se-crets," and another that says, "Here! Here, here, here!"

I could see the Disney connection and the video game as a sad commentary on my life. Why do the real sounds of nature make me think of unreal things? But yesterday I found the front entrance to the sanctuary and learned that this is one of the top four locations in the entire United States for bird viewing.

So yes, the number of birds here is unreal, if spectacular. And this isn't even the season for them. Their peaks are during spring and fall migrations, not mid-winter.

The dark spots on the sky are birds, beautiful to watch.

I've mostly abandoned my attempts to photograph them, though. Yesterday, I was on the beach at sunrise, trying to take a photo of one of the birds lifting off from the water.

The birds were dark against the rising sun, so graceful, so mystical, and there were so many of them. The sound of the waves was like the heartbeat of the world, punctuated by the cries of the birds. It was still, barely a breeze, and cold enough that I was bundled up, wearing my scarf and gloves and coat, but not so cold that I was uncomfortable. And Zelda was bouncing around like a puppy.

But I couldn't get a bird in a photo at all — they were too far away to be anything more than dark spots — and Zelda's tugging kept bumping my phone so my photos were blurry.

As I got frustrated, I realized that trying to save the memory was getting in the way of enjoying the sunrise and appreciating being on the beach with my dog, so I stopped trying.

I did take a few photos, today, though in a "lift the phone, click, see what it looks like later," mode. My new photography plan is to not put any effort into getting the perfect shot, just to take a bunch and hope to get lucky.

FEBRUARY 6, 2017 - TICKFAW STATE PARK, LOUISIANA

I woke up early this morning, maybe because I was hearing a weird noise — like a far-distant telephone dial, the old-fashioned rotary kind — but probably just because I went to bed really early last night.

It was 5AM or so and I spent the next half hour trying to track down the noise: moving around the van, opening windows to see if it was louder outside, turning off circuits from the circuit breaker, running the water, going outside and turning the water off — every new attempt punctuated by five minutes or so of trying to go back to sleep.

Finally I gave up and got up. It was a little after six. Sunrise was at six-forty, so it was still dark, but getting lighter, and Z was ready for her walk.

It was a gray and foggy morning. Mist was everywhere and it was doing that thing where even though it's not raining, the mist condenses on the tree leaves and then drips, so it sounded like there were tiny random footsteps happening all around me.

They weren't footsteps, of course, they were just drops of water hitting the ground. I'm a rational person, I know that's what that sound was.

Not footsteps, just water drops.

But we wandered along the road, down a short path to the deserted nature center, then down another road, and right to the edge of a boardwalk path into the woods.

And there I stopped.

These weren't exactly woods. Tickfaw State Park is a cypress swamp. The trees are probably beautiful in summer, but it's the middle of winter, so right now they're trunks of mostly bare gray branches, with scattered dead leaves hanging from them. Occasional scrub pines provide a bit of color, but the ground is dark and muddy, covered with leaves or swampy water.

The reason I stopped was because to the right of the boardwalk, in the swamp, there was a rustling. And then a sound like a coughing bark.

Not a bark, not a cough, but something in between.

It wasn't a sound that a squirrel makes, not a chitter or a squeak. It was a bigger sound than that. But it wasn't a rumble or a growl, either.

I told myself it was perfectly safe. I didn't know what was making that sound, but I wasn't going to walk into the swamp, I was going to walk on the boardwalk.

Zelda was tugging at the leash. She was quite eager to go sniff interesting smells.

I was not so sure.

And then, from the left, I heard a howl. A real, true, actual howl. Like a wolf howling at the moon howl.

Like a werewolf howl.

I was sure it was a coyote, equally sure it was far away.

And I was totally positive that the little footstep sounds I heard all around me were just water drips from the trees created by the mist. And whatever the thing coughing at me from the trees to the right was (probably a raccoon, right?), it was definitely not a monster from a shadow realm going to eat us both alive.

But I was not getting on that boardwalk, just not.

So Zelda and I walked back along the road and deeper into the park. I saw an owl fly across the road, and then fly from tree to tree until it disappeared into the swamp. I saw two snowy white egrets lift into the air, so beautiful and so ungainly. An entire flock of some much smaller bird flew so close overhead that I heard their wings beating.

Right now the park basically belongs to me and the birds. The campground has spots for thirty RVs; I believe there might be two other campers here. It is peaceful, serene, beautiful... and also quite spooky. In a mostly fun way.

This is the mist about half an hour later (and lighter) than when I decided, nope, not getting on that path.

FEBRUARY 9, 2017 - SAM HOUSTON JONES STATE PARK, LOUISIANA

Yesterday was the first day in a long while where I wrote no words for no reason. I wasn't traveling, I wasn't busy with other things, I had plenty of time, but I just didn't write.

I went to bed feeling bleak and annoyed with myself and woke up feeling miserably sick. I gave Zelda the shortest walk she's had in a while, then came back and crawled back under the covers.

This park feels much bigger and more urban than most of the places I've stayed recently. Partly it's that it's near a highway. Instead of birds and bugs and strange animals, there's traffic noise. Also, many picnic tables and a commensurate amount of litter.

My first afternoon here, I watched two big cats — house cats, not wild, but I'd guess feral — stalking through the forest out my window. They feel like the definition of the place: feral, not wild.

Example: this morning's walk, admittedly short, included an encounter with a half-dressed guy staggering along the trail. Not staggering in the "I'm an injured hiker" way, but staggering in the "drunk guy, sleeping it off in the woods" way. I didn't cut my walk short because of him, but it definitely lowers my enthusiasm for random strolls through deserted trails in the semi-dark.

It's quite sad how desperately I wish I was back in my house, in my comfortable bed, with my freezer full of homemade chicken stock and my electric tea kettle. And my fenced backyard, so the dogs could go out without me needing to drag myself out with them.

Also, I wish a guy with both technical competence and interest in fixing things like the stereo's inconsistent bluetooth and lousy sound quality would show up in my life.

But now I'm going to go write because daydreaming about the boy who's going to save me defeats the purpose of creating my own happy ever after.

Still, if wishes were horses, I'd have a full stable today.

FEBRUARY 14, 2017 - GALVESTON ISLAND STATE PARK, TEXAS

I love Galveston. The park has vast expanses of blackened land, presumably recovering from a controlled burn, with wild grasses growing and not much else. It's flat and muddy and dark. And by some standard, the weather has been terrible. I haven't seen a sunrise since I got here because it's been so foggy. But the fog isn't cold, it just has a hint of ocean chill and it smells like ocean.

Zelda and I have gotten muddy and sandy and wet and salty. (Bartleby, not so much, because he does the finicky dog thing of, "What? You want me to walk there? On THAT? No, thank you.")

It's delightful.

Sandy, muddy Zelda. We didn't see any alligators, though!

I could live without the tornado warnings, though. Today has been a non-stop stream of the national weather service letting me know that I'm going to die soon. Any minute now! Watching the ocean during a thunderstorm is great, though — the waves are impressive, but the flashes of lightning make them even better.

Despite the rain, I saw some gorgeous sunsets.

Of course, I'm hoping to avoid any actual tornados. I did unplug *Serenity* and move from the campsite to a parking lot, out of some notion of being ready to move should it be necessary, but I'm not sure how I would know it was actually necessary short of seeing a forming tornado.

Back to the park: there are birds I've never seen before, tall and short and in-between. One was a reddish egret, which I wouldn't know, except that I found a sign telling me so. Two yesterday were tall and pink and mysterious. I'm fairly sure – after abandoning all hope of conserving my internet data to research the question – that they were roseate spoonbills.

If you had told me six months ago that I was going to be so interested in birds that I would be looking for an app to help me identify them, I would have looked at you sideways, but there you go. One never knows what travel will offer.

FEBRUARY 16, 2017 - GALVESTON, TEXAS

I woke up this morning and thought, okay, it's time to move. It's my 6th day here, making this my longest stay in a state park. I've visited the little beach around the corner a few times every day, and I've walked along the road toward the front of the park every morning.

I was tired of it. Yesterday was cold and gray and I turned back when I started to feel raindrops, so I was decidedly unenthusiastic about doing the same walk one more time.

An hour later, I was in love with Galveston again.

Instead of walking toward the front of the park, we took a different road and I found a trail that led into the park and out into the grass. It was a half mile loop, with an observation stand at the end, where you could climb up and look out over the water where tons of white birds were floating and stalking around.

I couldn't believe I hadn't found it earlier in the week.

I took a lot of blurry pictures of birds, too, but this shows the expanse, the sense of spaciousness.

I'm still getting used to living in *Serenity*. I'm still finding ways to make life easier, things to change. I bought $20 worth of plastic storage containers a few weeks ago and threw out all the random containers I had, so now my containers stack. It felt so wasteful and sounds so trivial, but wow, what a difference to not have dishes falling on my head when I open the cabinets.

On the same extravagant day, I bought liquid soap and threw away my bar soap and its holder. Bar soap is just not worth the effort; it gets too messy.

I've finally figured out where it's best to keep my toothbrush, at least for now. (Inside a cup, in the medicine cabinet.)

I'm even getting the hang of washing dishes using the least possible amount of water. I found a collapsible dish pan that fits inside the sink. When I'm being careful about water, I use spray bottles, one with hot soapy water and the other with rinsing water, and when I don't need to be quite so careful, I fill the sink with a couple inches of hot soapy water, and use the dishpan for rinsing.

One of the trickiest things to figure out, though, is how long to spend in any one place. Traveling too fast is so disruptive that I get no writing done. Traveling too slow and the van starts to feel like a trap.

I think, though, that I may have mixed up traveling too slow with staying in the wrong places. Two weeks in a campground where my view is other people's sewer lines may be very different from two weeks in a place where six days in I can still be surprised by beauty.

FEBRUARY 20, 2017 - MATAGORDA BAY, TEXAS

I sang while walking Zelda yesterday morning.

Yep, singing in public. Loudly, too.

Except it wasn't really public. We were on a completely deserted beach, ocean pounding away, with the sun peeking out from behind clouds, with that sort of celestial rays of light thing happening. Singing felt totally appropriate.

I should probably learn either a few more songs or the actual lyrics of "Joy to the World" if I intend to continue singing while walking the dog, though, because my singing involved a fair amount of "something, something, something," lyrics.

When I first got to this campground, on Friday, I'd been driving in the rain for a while and I was so tired of rain. After living in Florida and California for most of the past 25 years, I forgot that in some places rain just goes on and on and on.

Not that I would have expected Texas to be one of those places, but hey, live and learn.

The campground wasn't my favorite but the beach was fantastic.

The campground is a parking lot, with rows of RVs. They're nice spaces, with plenty of room between sites, concrete picnic tables, and smooth large driveways, but what I can see out of my windows – front, back, both sides – is another camper. It's not cozy. Combine that with the rain and I was less than enthusiastic.

But the campground borders the southern end of the Colorado River and miles and miles of true ocean beach. Sitting in the camper is not so interesting, but the walking is fantastic.

A long jetty made of metal grating goes out over the water. At the end, you can feel the spray, hear the crashing waves, and look down at the water, probably at least ten feet below you. It's exhilarating in the way the ocean can be, like you're breathing pure freedom.

The beach has lots of shells, so the beachcombing is fun, but best of all, when I asked the campground host about letting dogs off leash, she shrugged, and said, "Sure, no one cares." Yay!

Sadly, it continues to rain. I turned the heater on in the van and I'm trying to pretend that I'm in a cozy nest, instead of feeling like I'm camping in the rain.

I'm struggling with the dilemma of accumulating wet things, though. There's no way for anything to get dry, short of finding a laundromat. And everything is starting to feel damp.

I need some sunshine.

MARCH 2, 2017 - PALMETTO STATE PARK, TEXAS

At the Onion River Campground in Vermont, I walked Zelda through fields of high, dry weeds with scattered faded flowers, surrounded by deep green grass and trees with leaves that were just starting to hint at autumn, and felt like we were in the essence of late summer. I think it's why I remember that place with so much pleasure.

At Palmetto State Park in Texas, we are in the essence of spring. It is pure spring, all around us. Trees with soft green leaves unfurling, growing so fast that it feels like if you look away for an instant they will have changed when you look back.

Wildflowers — yellow and white and purple and pink — some tiny, hiding in the grass, others standing tall and proud.

A robin sitting on the branch outside my window as I write.

White-tailed deer leaping through the trees at sunrise.

Sweet olive trees covered in white flowers, their fragrance drifting on the breeze. One of the sweet olive trees — the biggest one I've ever seen — hummed as I approached it, mysterious until I realized it was the hum of a thousand happy bees. (I then cautiously moved away because, okay, humming tree, fascinating and cool; hundreds upon hundreds of bees, totally scary.)

My day here yesterday was... I want to say spectacular, but it was spectacular in a really quiet way. Zelda and I walked the San Marcos River Trail a little after sunrise. It was a perfect morning walk, chilly enough to need a jacket, overcast, but not raining, a good length, interesting things to look at.

I did some work, including updating my work blog, texted with some friends, did some knitting, made myself a delicious lunch — scrambled eggs with chorizo, brown rice, goat Gouda, avocado, mushroom, and green onion — and ate it sitting outside looking at the view. The sky was clearing, and the air was warming.

Then Z and I went for another walk, in a different direction. We crossed the river at a low point, which for her meant wading and for me meant hopping along the stones at the edges of the paved walkway, the rest of which had water flowing across it. I felt slightly ridiculous and yet also had that little kid thrill of knowing that if I fell, I would splash.

Back at the camper, I wrote. Good words. First time in a long while that I didn't feel like I was trying to fix something broken, but just letting the characters be who they were. We went for another walk. I sat outside on my new camp chair ($6 at Walmart and so much more comfortable than the $50 backpacking chair that I started out with) in the sunshine, warm enough to not need my jacket, and tried to write some more. Then Zelda wanted to be on my lap, so instead I snuggled her and felt so grateful to be in that moment, in that chair, with my dog licking my face. At sunset, we went for another walk. We ate dinner. I wrote some more.

Then I heard a rustling and discovered a mouse in my trash can. Ack! I carried it outside and released it, telling it to watch out for owls. Unfortunately, it was either not the only mouse or it came right back inside, because there was one after my granola this morning. Ugh.

But I didn't let the mice stress me out yesterday. Yesterday, I enjoyed a perfect spring day. And not just a perfect spring day. My day, the day that I wanted.

A year ago, I was just starting to think about this adventure. I hadn't decided to do it yet. I could still look around my house and think, wait, this is the home that I worked so hard for, the place where I wanted to live forever, my fantasy house. The window seat with its cushion made from material my mom and I found at a garage sale, the French doors, the bougainvillea, the neighborhood with its ponds and birds, the kitchen that is *exactly* right... was I really going to let it all go?

Yesterday was the day for which I let it go.

MARCH 4, 2017 - BRAZOS BEND, TEXAS

I spent one night at Brazos Bend. I'm starting to believe that one night isn't enough for any park, but it's especially not enough for one as big as Brazos Bend. So many trails! So many things to see! An observatory and a windmill and multiple lakes. I'm not even sure what I might have missed.

Well, except for the alligators – based on the warnings, I should definitely have seen some alligator activity, but our one morning there was cold so there was no sign of them. I don't actually mind that.

We did see vultures. Lots of vultures. Zelda and I startled about a dozen of them while we were out walking. They'd been hidden in the brush and I hadn't noticed them, but we were so close that the sound of their wings beating the air as they leaped into flight was incredibly loud, like a motor suddenly starting right next to you. I ducked, heart abruptly racing. Zelda was totally nonchalant, of course, but vultures are big when you're only a few feet away from them.

The plants were loud, too. The wind blowing through them was a steady rustle, like... I don't know what. Maybe I don't have a comparison. They sounded papery, but loud papery, like dozens of people all reading newspapers at once, making no other sounds, no clearing of breath or shifting weight, just shuffling their papers around. I'm not musical enough to be sure, but I bet there's some musical instrument that could replicate the sound. I'd never heard anything like it before, though.

Traveling like this is making me feel incredibly ignorant. About so many things! Musical instruments at the moment, but birds, of course. Plant life. I have no idea of the names of any of the wildflowers I've been admiring. The stars are an almost complete mystery, after I've found Orion's Belt and hunted for the Little Dipper.

These were the loud plants. I have no idea what they are.

Then there's geography. Matagorda Bay was at the end of the Colorado River. In Texas. This was completely mystifying until I finally googled and discovered that Texas' Colorado River is not the same river as the Colorado River that runs through the Grand Canyon. (And, random new fact, Colorado means "red" in Spanish. I had no idea.)

MARCH 7, 2017 - GALVESTON BEACH, TEXAS

It's a measure of my mood yesterday that I walked along the beach thinking about how beaches are really just big cemeteries.

Sand? Just the decayed and crumbled skeletons of sea creatures.

Shells? Leftover body parts.

Dying jellyfish? Well, you know, dying jellyfish.

I was glad that I'd already read online that there's no point in trying to save the jellyfish because otherwise I might have felt I should try. But a) they might sting you and b) the conditions that caused them to wash up on shore still exist, so they'll be back onshore soon even if you do manage to get them into the ocean.

And c) there were far too many of them. I know if I'd managed to save one that it might have appreciated it, but I would have felt overwhelmed by the futility. And probably stung, too.

On the other hand, gorgeous beach! Big shells! Beautiful dying jellyfish in iridescent greens and blues.

As dying things go, the jellyfish were remarkably beautiful.

And the weather's been crap — I swear, Texas might be the wettest state I have ever spent time in — but the sun came out twice, once at sunset last night, and then this morning for about an hour, just long enough for Zelda and me to have a walk.

I think my mood has been shaded by the mice, too. I'm not even sure I can explain how oppressive I find it to be living with something I'm trying to kill.

At this point, I've captured and released one, killed another, and spent about $45 in anti-mice devices. I have ultrasonic repellers plugged into three different outlets, traps baited with "mouse attractor" in two locations, peppermint oil sprayed along the floor, dryer sheets in the drawers, and the whole van smells like Christmas from the FreshCab mouse repellent. I feel like I should be putting up lights and baking cookies.

I'm not a vegetarian, so I don't know why I feel so guilty about killing a mouse. But I hate this. It makes me simultaneously sad and jumpy, paranoid that every sound is a mouse getting near my bed and that every sniffle is the first symptom of a mouse-born virus.

Galveston Beach

MARCH 15, 2017 - SANDERS COVE, TEXAS

On Sunday, I was chatting with R and he asked me how I was doing.

I opened my mouth to answer, "Great," and instead, "I'm really getting tired of camping," slipped out.

There was a pause.

And then he said, ever so politely, "How unfortunate."

I laughed.

Yes, it is unfortunate to get tired of camping when one lives in a camper. I wrote to a friend recently that I'm one of those sensible campers who, when it gets too uncomfortable, says, "Okay, it's time to go home now."

Ah, yes, home. That would be right where I am, right? Which at the time was a crowded campground in the dreary rain.

Fortunately, yesterday I left said campground and headed north. I was a little worried about the drive: I've been aiming for two hours between destinations, but yesterday was five. I shouldn't have worried.

Five hours is actually better than two, I think, because somewhere past two hours but before three, I hit the fun driving zone where being on the road started to feel like an adventure again. I was driving through cute little Texas towns — Athens, Paris — and along roads with real ranches.

In Paris, I stopped for groceries. Google let me know that I had a choice between two local stores or Walmart, so of course I went to one of the local stores.

Wrong choice, I guess, but at least I didn't need much. The dog food was $16.99 (instead of the $12.99 I usually pay); the only gluten-free granola was actually Chex Mix; and I should have read the label on the yogurt before I bought it because I took one bite this morning, and only then discovered that the second ingredient is sugar.

Oh, well. It was still fun. In the past month, I've been to Trader Joe's, Costco, and Walmart, because they had things that I needed or wanted. But they're all alike. Trader Joe's in Texas might as well be Trader Joe's in Florida or in California.

Wandering around someplace different was good for me.

Post grocery store, I continued north to my campground. It's my first Army Corps of Engineers campground and what a pleasant surprise.

I'm not particularly good at researching my campground destinations. It takes a ton of time, it uses up my precious internet data at an appalling rate, and I haven't figured out my priorities yet. Does a good view beat a level spot? Sometimes. Is proximity to the showers good or bad? It depends. Almost everything feels like "it depends" to me, except space between campers (the more the better) and access to nature.

I would never have figured out how nice this campground was from the internet because one of its advantages is that it's really hilly. The sites are terraced up the hill, so that they all get a wonderful view of the lake. Last night, my neighbors down the hill from me were sitting out around their table, chatting with one another. I felt silly as I kept opening the window to take picture after picture of the scene behind them, because they were looking toward me. But I also wanted to call down to them, "turn around, turn around, look at what's behind you."

It was the most beautiful sunset I'd seen in weeks of gorgeous sunsets.

95

Last night, I left all the windows in the van uncovered. In most campgrounds, it feels vulnerable to be sitting in the camper with the darkness all around me. When it gets dark, I put the covers over the windshield and front windows, close the blinds on the kitchen window, pull down the shades over the side windows, hang up a magnetic curtain over the sliding door window, and pull the shower curtain in the back. It's part of the evening routine, usually done before washing all the dishes and taking the trash out.

But I didn't bother last night. Instead I went to sleep looking at the stars in the black sky, between the bare branches of trees.

So this morning — ridiculously early — I woke up when it got light. Not light because of the sunrise, light because of the full moon. Zelda thought it was probably time to get up and it took me a while to convince her that no, we were not going outside in the not-quite-freezing cold to walk.

I nearly wrote "walk in the dark" but it wasn't dark. The light wasn't warm, it was a cool blue light, but it was definitely bright enough that we could have wandered around the campground without worrying about tripping or running into things.

When we finally did get up, at sunrise instead of moonrise, the moon was still in the sky. So were huge flocks of birds. Hundreds of them flew overhead, close enough that I could hear the beating of their wings, like taffeta rustling. They were quacky birds, not cheeping or trilling, but I don't think they were ducks.

Between the sunset, the stars, the moon, the birds, the water — well, and most likely, the fact that it did not rain yesterday and might not today either — I am, at least for the moment, no longer tired of camping.

MARCH 19, 2017 - LAKE CATHERINE, ARKANSAS

I'm sitting outside, computer in my lap, both dogs roaming around in the piles of dead leaves around me. The sun is shining, there's a cool breeze off the lake blowing wisps of hair into my face, the birds are incredibly noisy, and I'm feeling supremely content.

Yesterday, I left Oklahoma and took the scenic Talimena Highway to Arkansas. The first part was by far the most exciting: the road that my GPS took me down — well, up, really — was a logging road.

Dirt and gravel, narrow and steep. It was ten minutes of thinking, "Oh, shit, what happens if I run into someone else on this road?"

And then I did run into someone else. Fortunately, I was on the side that could tuck into the hill, so I pulled over as far as I could and they passed by on the scarier side, waving at me as they did. But the adrenaline and the excitement and the sheer fun of the uncertainty was great.

I was worried that the road would come to an abrupt end, and I'd have to turn around or back all the way down. Backing down would have been a nightmare. But instead it let me out onto this itty-bitty two-lane road, which turned out to be the scenic highway. I was so pleased.

I stopped at a bunch of scenic vistas and took pictures of clouds. Look, more clouds! I had just enough glimpses beyond the clouds that it was obvious that it was a pretty road. In better weather. Someday I'll try again.

Arkansas, meanwhile, has been delightful. I emerged from the clouds into sunshine and spring. For a lot of the drive, the trees alongside the road were simultaneously autumn and spring — trees that hadn't lost their orange and red leaves from fall yet, interspersed with pink blossoming trees.

I wound up coming down to Hot Springs, and then beyond to Lake Catherine State Park. The park had one campsite available, for four days, so I took it. And here I sit, ridiculously cheerful.

It's the sun, I think. Well, and also, the campground is packed with happy families having fun camping, which is enjoyable to listen to. There's water and trails, and people with boats, and kids on bikes and skateboards and it feels like... Spring? Vacation?

Joy.

It feels like joy.

Last night, I sat in *Serenity* watching other people's flickering campfires and smelling wood smoke and appreciating the bare branches of trees against the dark sky with its sprinkling of stars. This morning, the sunrise was golden-orange against the same dark branches.

I couldn't find gluten-free granola in any of my most recent stores, so I'm baking some of my own and the van smells delicious, like baked oats and cinnamon. I've got a Verizon signal, but no T-mobile, so my internet is limited, but I'll still be able to talk to R today. The previous campers left behind a rawhide chew, so Z is having a good time burying it in the leaves, then moving it to another spot and burying it again.

All these little random pieces, they add up to happiness.

MARCH 22, 2017 - LAKE CATHERINE, ARKANSAS

I have to leave Lake Catherine today.

I would rather not.

I would like to move in here, to sit in my campsite and listen to the kids playing (so many kids! so much laughter!), to wander around the park and hike on its trails and kayak on its lake for, I don't know, forever?

I guess I'd get bored eventually. But I haven't even done the hard hikes yet. And I only kayaked once!

I'm not sure how the past three days passed so quickly. They were the kind of days where one moment flows seamlessly into the next, where you never think, "What should I do now?" because there always feels like an obvious next thing to do.

Obvious next things included some cooking: the aforementioned granola; a mushroom and asparagus omelette with hollandaise sauce; spicy veggie hash topped with a fried egg; grilled chicken breast marinated in yogurt and herbs on mixed greens; and chicken salad with veggies and lime. Also delicious cantaloupe with prosciutto; strawberries and yogurt with my granola every morning; and baby carrots and celery with avocado ranch dressing for snacks.

Yes, I ate well.

I mostly do anyway, but there's a correlation for me between cooking creatively and happiness, and I'm not sure which way it flows.

Was I happy because I was cooking creatively or was I cooking because I was happy? Maybe it's one of those circular things, where feeling cheerful inspired me to create something delicious which then made me happy to eat and so on. At any rate, the happiness/food circle was in full flow.

Another obvious next thing was some cleaning. The pollen is such that everything gets coated with a sheen of yellow powder in about two hours, so I've been steadily dusting. But also I desperately need to do laundry, so I took the opportunity of having an almost empty clothes cupboard to clean and re-organize. I was grateful to find no sign of mice.

I also washed the incredibly dirty van, most of it with just a jug of water, no soap, and a dishcloth that is never going to be clean again, but all the windows with Windex. Plus swept and washed dishes, rearranged the dog's beds, changed the sheets — the usual cleaning.

Lots of walks, mostly with Zelda, but some with B, too. Mostly just meandering around the campground, but Z and I hiked on the two mile trail on Sunday and it was terrific. It was hilly and narrow, running along a stream, with occasional bits steep enough or slippery enough that I regretted wearing sandals instead of hiking boots.

About halfway through Zelda was done, so I had to persuade her along, walking out to the end of her leash, then crouching until she came to me, rubbing her ears and telling her how good she was, then doing the same thing all over again. Possibly I should not have made that our third walk of the day.

Eventually, the path led to a small waterfall with lots of kids playing. Zelda walked in the water for a while and perked right up. At the end of the trail a wobbly bridge reminded me of Tom Sawyer's island.

In fact, this park in general reminds me of Tom Sawyer's island. There are packs of kids running around everywhere — also biking, skateboarding, scootering — and they're so cute. One of my neighbors has that perfect kid laugh, an uninhibited gurgle of joy. I love the sound.

Possibly one of my very favorite things about Arkansas is that a great many small boys, ranging from reasonably little — 4? — to reasonably big — 12?, inform me that they like my dogs. They'll be walking by or riding their bikes and they don't say hi or anything, they just call out, "I like your dogs!"

After the fourth or fifth time, I finally settled on my response, which is to call back, "Thank you, I do, too!" But it is so endearing.

And today I kayaked. I brought Zelda with me, and made her wear her life jacket. She was not sure about the kayak for a while, but eventually she settled into hanging over the side, her front paws in the water, and let me paddle. It was gloriously beautiful. At one point, a butterfly fluttered by — yellow and black, not one that I recognized — and I thought, "I am on a lake. In Arkansas. Kayaking. With butterflies."

Which sure seems like stating the obvious, except — I'm in Arkansas! I feel like I should be pinching myself regularly. Not that Arkansas was some dream destination of mine, but it's beautiful.

I think it's more that I can't believe this is my life right now.

One of the waterfalls we found.

MARCH 27, 2017 - GUNTER HILL, ALABAMA

From the van window, I see trees and river beyond them, in one of the loveliest views I've had in a while. The Army Corps of Engineers are good at laying out campgrounds.

Obviously, not every site can be great, but this campground has the sites positioned so that even though there are campers on either side of me, none of us are blocking the others' views of the river.

I'm baking granola again. This time I added sliced almonds, took out the dates, upped the cinnamon, and added some salt. I think I upped the coconut oil inadvertently, but I suspect that if I'm really going to start making my own granola, I'll be playing with this recipe.

And I think I probably am going to start making my own granola. While I'm not sure there's any economic advantage — the ingredients are still not cheap — I like the control. Every morning... hmm, this story requires more background.

So I have a theory about happiness. Actually, I have many theories about happiness. But this theory is relevant to granola.

I believe that happiness is woven from four threads: awareness, acceptance, appreciation, and anticipation, and that it's something you can get better at with practice. When I eat breakfast in the morning, I like to practice.

Yes, I practice happiness. I know it sounds ridiculous. Bear with me.

I mostly eat yogurt with granola and fruit for breakfast. When you eat the same thing every day, it's easy to stop noticing it. Who pauses to savor the familiar, after all?

But that makes breakfast a good chance to practice happiness. Before I take that first bite, I try to remember to anticipate: is this going to be good yogurt? Will it blend well with the granola? How are those blueberries going to taste?

As I take the first few bites, I try to be aware of them, to experience them fully. To notice if the yogurt is the perfect blend of tangy and sweet, or not. To feel the blueberries in my mouth and their burst of flavor. To acknowledge the crunch of the granola, its texture on my tongue and cheeks, its taste.

And then I try to accept whatever the reality is, and appreciate it no matter what. Maybe the blueberries aren't the best. They're out of season and their flavor is bland, or they're over-ripe and squishy. But still, even not-very-good blueberries are a luxury, a fresh taste that I'm lucky to have.

Then I get to anticipate tomorrow's breakfast, when maybe I'll have a different fruit, maybe banana or strawberries.

And yes, the cynic in me finds this entirely silly.

But the me that's living my life — the me that's choosing to be happy — has discovered that starting the day by practicing happiness with breakfast makes for good days. I like beginning my day with a buzz of contentment flowing through me, a reminder of pleasure and joy.

But I actually like it a lot better when the three pieces of my breakfast are good. When my thoughts are more, "Oh, yum, I love this yogurt, this is so delicious," rather than "Huh, I wonder how much sugar is in this, I should have read the label, but I will do my best to appreciate it nonetheless."

It's all well and good to practice happiness, but it's so much easier to do a good job at it when the ingredients position me for success.

Back to granola: I'm not sure how many different granolas I've tried over the past six months. Ten? Twelve? I almost never buy the same one twice, because they've all got good parts and bad parts. I did throw away one I truly disliked, because being smart about happiness does mean changing things that flat-out don't work.

But getting good at happiness isn't about finding perfection in life, it's about appreciating what I have.

Mostly the granola is neutral in my breakfast, there because I need the calories to keep me going through the morning. The granola I made, though, became something to think about.

My appreciation was lukewarm. The oats were flaky, somehow. They had a texture that wasn't quite finished. But they improved as they got stale, so maybe I just needed to bake them longer. And the dates were terrible, so solid that they crunched instead of being chewy. Plus it was missing something, which I finally realized was a sprinkle of salt.

By the time I finished the granola, this morning, it had gotten really good, maybe not the best granola I'd eaten in the past six months, but close. (I picked out the dates and added salt, as well as the aforementioned staleness.)

So yeah, wasn't that a long-winded way of saying that I think I'll keep making granola?

In my practice of happiness, it tilts the odds in my favor to love my breakfast, to start the day thinking, "Wow, that was excellent," and to have my appreciation be about the greatness of the experience, rather than how fortunate I am to have the first-world problem of not loving my fresh fruit.

I've been living in *Serenity* for eight months now, and they've flown by.

They've not been un-stressful. Things have gone wrong, it's been a huge adjustment, and I'm still working on how to live more comfortably in such a small and mobile space.

A cool bridge at Gunter Hill

But this month as a whole feels like the month where it all came together, where an awful lot of the time I lived in a continual state of awareness, acceptance, appreciation, and anticipation.

In other words, happiness.

ON PRACTICING HAPPINESS

Here's something I know about happiness: if you're searching for it, you'll never find it.

It's a catch-22. The act of searching is inherently unhappy. Searching means you're dissatisfied. Searching is frustrating. It doesn't matter how you define happiness or what you think will you bring you happiness or how you're looking for it. As long as you want what you don't have — as long as you're looking — you aren't happy. They're mutually exclusive states.

Here's another thing I know about happiness: life is challenging. Life has ups and downs, good and bad. Life has pain and loss, grief and suffering, hardship and injustice.

If you're always happy in the face of those things, you're probably an asshole.

Here's a third thing I know: happiness is a choice.

I practice it, because I'm not very good at it. It doesn't come naturally to me. If I believed the set point theory of happiness, which states that our happiness level is hard-wired, my dial would be set on anxiety and depression.

But I don't believe in the set point theory.

I work at happiness, because I believe — in fact, I know — that I'm happier when I make the effort to be so. When I pause and pay attention to my feelings and the world around me. When I acknowledge my feelings honestly and accept them. When I look for reasons to be grateful and appreciative. When I re-frame and look forward with optimism.

Awareness, acceptance, appreciation, anticipation.

When I do those things, I — well, have a better chance of being happy than when I don't.

I considered ending this memoir here, at this moment of happiness in Alabama. Doesn't it seem like an obvious conclusion?

But my van life didn't stop here.

I kept going.

II

HIGHLIGHTS AND LOW POINTS

6

THE REST OF 2017

At the end of May, I drove from Florida to Pennsylvania again. It was the same drive I made last year, with my house closing behind me, and *Serenity* overflowing with stuff.

This time the stuff was everything left from my storage unit: a cedar chest, a chair, plastic crates holding my grandma's china and R's childhood.

And overflowing was no exaggeration. A leg on the cedar chest broke when we were moving it into the van, so its contents were in another plastic crate and the bed was piled high. I had a sliver on which to sleep, small enough that rolling over meant bumping into a crate.

But my attitude was not at all the same. Last year, I was still running down checklists in my head, tight with tension and uncertainty. I was excited, but even finding a campground for the night felt like a challenge.

I vividly remember stopping at a rest stop and having that, "We're not in Kansas anymore," feeling because the air smelled different.

Ten months later, it felt familiar.

I didn't bother with a campground: I drove until it was almost dark, then found myself a quiet corner of a Flying J parking lot and settled in for the night.

It was actually only my second night in a real parking lot, and my first night on a highway parking lot, but I've spent enough time camped in driveways and on streets now that it didn't faze me. I just crawled into bed, apologized to B, who had to sleep on the floor, and crashed.

At 5AM Monday, I woke up and started driving again.

The house isn't livable, but I could park Serenity on the grass.

Several years ago, my brother bought an old stone farmhouse for the sake of the land around it. It's in a strange location, not exactly rural, not exactly suburban. Costco and Whole Foods are a mile away, across a highway, and it's on a road simultaneously too busy and too narrow to feel safe for walking. The house is not livable, although it could be amazing with a lot of work and probably a ton of money.

Right now, I intend to stay here until I finish writing the book I'm working on. Probably with some interruptions — I've got some fun weekends planned, spending time with friends and relatives — but mostly, I'm going to sit and write and watch the blueberries get ripe.

JUNE 19, 2017 - ALLENTOWN, PENNSYLVANIA

The fireflies were out last night. I had a moment of blinking disbelief — What was that light? Was I really seeing what I was seeing? — and then I realized what they were. Tiny yellow sparks in shadowy darkness, flickering in and out, in a warm summer breeze. A magical element of a Pennsylvania summer.

Some of the blueberries are ripe. So are the blackberries. So are the red raspberries. So are the yellow raspberries. The gooseberries and the grapes are not.

It's fun to watch the berries ripen — the blueberries, in particular, grow in a cluster, all of which get ripe at different times, so the cluster has berries ranging from deep blue to green.

And the blackberries get ripe so fast! Seriously, I could pick berries from a vine in the morning and then go back a few hours later and pick more. I can't quite see them changing color, but I bet if I set up a time-lapse camera, I could.

Unfortunately, it's also hot and sticky. I love camping here, but I keep looking at the house and contemplating how much work it would take to make it livable. Do you suppose it's possible to put central air-conditioning into a stone farmhouse? I guess anything's possible if you have enough money, which means I should not be wasting my time imagining renovating the house, but instead should be writing, writing, writing.

JUNE 29, 2017 - ALLENTOWN, PENNSYLVANIA

Happy Birthday, *Serenity*!

Technically, of course, her birthday must have been a couple months ago. She would have been built in Iowa, shipped to Florida, and she sat on the dealer's lot for at least a couple of weeks before I signed the papers. But one year ago today was the day she came home with me.

Of course, the very next day, I brought her back to the dealer and said, "Um, I don't think water is supposed to pour in through the roof when it rains," but that's neither here nor there.

It would still be close to another month before I closed on my house and started traveling, but here's what I've learned in my first year of van life.

1) Temperature control is a perpetual challenge. It easily gets about ten degrees hotter inside the van than it is outside, which is fine when it's 60 degrees outside and not fun at all when it's 80 degrees outside.

I've learned some tricks — always put the window covers up and the shades down, close the bathroom doors when the AC is on — but long-term, I also need to invest in some curtains to close off the cab and some USB fans to improve air flow. And I need to plan my travels better so I can avoid places and times where the heat is dangerous for the dogs.

2) Campgrounds are dirty. The dogs don't care. I do. I'm getting better at acceptance, but clean sheets have become a luxurious treat.

3) I don't need much stuff, but the stuff I do own grows to fill the available room. It feels like a continual process of pruning.

4) I expected that my eating habits would change, but I didn't know how. It turns out that I eat a lot of cold, fairly simple food — roast beef rolled up with arugula, turkey topped with artichoke spread, that kind of thing. Also, a lot more eggs.

But the longer I live in the van, the less limited I feel about what I can cook. I'm not sure I could do a Thanksgiving dinner, but short of that, I can cook some serious meals. When I'm not worried about heating up the van, that is.

5) Time flies by when you're living in a van. I really can't believe it's been a year. I thought back then that by now I might have figured out where I want to live and be ready to settle down somewhere — a year sounds like plenty of time to be living on the road, doesn't it? — but I'm nowhere close. I've enjoyed these past weeks of sitting still, but I'm looking forward to many more cautious adventures.

I guess I don't have any particularly profound insights.
A few more: birds are cool and worth watching.

Sea birds near Sarasota.

Also, I like sunrises better than sunsets; grocery stores are pretty much the same across the country; and I should stop waiting to do things, like put up curtains, with the idea that I'll do them when I get home because I am home.

Okay, one insight (still not terribly profound, I expect): a year ago, I plunged into the unknown. I was excited and I was scared. I scurried around with lists and to-do items and schedules and structure to try to cope with the vast looming uncertainties. I avoided thinking too far ahead even as I contemplated destinations like the Grand Canyon and Mount Rushmore. I was sure that there would be good parts and bad parts, and I tried not to focus too much on the possible bad parts.

It was a risk worth taking.

This journey, this life, this year has been amazing. It's not always comfortable and it's not always easy and yes, stuff has gone wrong and there have been some bad days along the way, but the good has so outweighed the bad.

My aunt sent me a quote this week with a note that said, "This is you." The quote was from Howard Thurman, who wrote:

Don't ask what the world needs. Ask what makes you come alive and go out and do it. Because what the world needs is people who have come alive.

Yes.

I didn't know a year ago that that's what I was doing, and that this journey would be as much about celebrating my breakfast every morning as it would be about visiting national parks — well, actually more about the former, since I have yet to set foot in a single national park, ha — but yes.

Letting go of my house and my stuff and my routine has been like waking up to a life of wonder and appreciation.

It wasn't the best decision of my life (which is an honor forever and always reserved to my response when faced with an unplanned, terribly-timed pregnancy), but it comes really close.

So, yeah, Happy Birthday, *Serenity*! May we celebrate many more together.

JULY 14, 2017 - BLACK MOSHANNON STATE PARK, PA

Bugs.

Allergies.

Rain.

No internet or cell connection, except for fleeting moments of a moving Verizon signal that disappears almost immediately.

No water at the campsite.

Ten miles up a steep and winding road, away from grocery stores and other conveniences.

At $31/night, not cheap. In fact, by my standards, reasonably expensive.

And did I mention the bugs? Not just mosquitoes and ticks, but these buzzing flies that dive bomb my head, seeming to try to get into my ears. I told myself I was being paranoid, that it was just the way they fly, but after multiple unpleasant walks, really, I think they're trying to get into my ears. They are madly annoying!

Speaking of paranoia, based mostly on the posted signs, I've been worried about four things here.

In order of probability:

1. Poison ivy
2. Lyme disease
3. Someone scolding me for walking my dog in the wrong place
4. Encountering a black bear

In order of danger/potential damage:

1. Lyme disease
2. Encountering a black bear
3. Poison ivy
4. Someone scolding me for walking my dog in the wrong place

In order of how much I've worried:

1. Someone scolding me for walking my dog in the wrong place
2. ... tied for a distant 2nd: poison ivy, Lyme disease, black bears.

Seriously, sometimes my brain annoys me.

I suppose it's good that I'm not obsessing on black bears, but the posted pet rules say there are off-limit areas for pets. The only one I've seen is the playground. On every walk, between trying to wave off bugs and covering my ears, I've wondered whether I've missed a sign and some ranger is going to appear out of nowhere and tell me I shouldn't be where I am. And if one did? So what! It's not like it would result in days of itching or emergency room visits or a life-changing, debilitating illness. And yet I worry anyway.

What a waste of energy.

The park is actually beautiful. The campground is thoroughly forested, the kind of place where you can envision black bears and other wildlife happily roaming. A short walk away, there's a dark lake with a sandy beach and a swimming area marked with buoys. Kayak rentals are $12/hour, $10 if you pay cash.

On my first day here, I thought it would be a great place to bring my niece next summer, but then the bugs started attacking and I thought better of it. But I do think in a different mood or in a different time of year, I'd like this place a lot more. Maybe just a better bug repellent would do it.

The best part of it, for me, has been hours spent writing. Rainy days + unpleasant walks + no internet = plenty of time spent staring at the computer screen.

JULY 21, 2017 - SOMEWHERE IN PENNSYLVANIA

In 18 states and two territories (one American and one British), I stayed in 73 different places:

- 25 state parks
- 13 driveways
- 12 Thousand Trails campgrounds
- 4 independent campgrounds
- 4 Passport America campgrounds
- 2 KOA campgrounds
- 2 Army Corps of Engineers campgrounds
- 2 parking lots
- 2 hotels
- 2 houses
- 1 Lower Colorado River Authority Park
- 1 USDA Forest Service campground
- 1 county park

- 1 Harvest Hosts site
- ... and one sailboat

I definitely got my money's worth from my Thousand Trails membership. I think my total spent is currently about $550 for about 80 days, so roughly $7/night. But I'm not going to be renewing it when it expires next year: those campgrounds seem like good places for families with small kids and people who are looking for stable bases for extended periods, but that's not how I want to travel or live.

My KOA membership was not worth the money. Again, great for families with kids and I definitely enjoyed the really nice showers at the KOA in Bellefonte, but I don't need the amenities they offer and even with the reduced membership rate, they were some of the most expensive places I stayed.

Passport America costs around $45/year and I bought a three-year membership, so I've got plenty of time for it to pay off. In fact, the park at which I'm currently staying is both a state park and a Passport America park, and I saved $14 on an upcoming night's stay because of my PA membership, so yay. But I've got a long way to go before that membership pays for itself. Two of the parks on the PA list were among my least favorite of the places I've stayed, so I don't seek them out. I should though, because it's a nice discount when the park is okay.

Generally speaking, the worthwhile memberships for me were the state parks. I've got a Texas State Park pass and a Georgia State Park pass and they were both good deals, worth the price.

Live and learn, right?

I can't believe I haven't stayed in a single national park — what kind of camper am I? — but they're more restrictive about dogs than state parks, and I've enjoyed discovering the state parks. Still, that might be a goal for Year Two.

I budgeted $900/month for campground charges, figuring an average of $30/night. If I regularly stayed at KOAs and independent campgrounds or even some of the more expensive state parks, I'd be breaking that budget on a regular basis. As it is, however, my blend of campgrounds and driveways kept me under budget every month.

I budgeted $400/month for gas and propane and I came in under budget on that, too, although that's obviously affected by where I'm going and how much I'm driving. I foresee breaking it when I drive cross-country.

My grocery budget was not good. Eating the way I eat — heavy on vegetables and protein, almost non-existent on breads, pasta, grains — is not cheap. Since I can't buy in bulk and store leftovers in my freezer, I'm spending more on food than I like.

The dogs were also way over budget. No surprise, but ouch. Even hiding some of their food costs in my grocery budget, I spent over $300/month on them. I'd budgeted $90. I guess two aging dogs don't come cheap. Still, the only way that number goes down is bad, so the positive side of breaking my budget on pet care is that I have two dogs I adore.

Health insurance and care, internet, auto and RV insurance, the storage unit, taxes: none of those were surprising numbers to me, although they do add up. Life in the van is less expensive than it was in my house, but I'd hoped I'd have a book or two released by now, so that's not so good.

But there, goals for Year Two — publish books and visit national parks!

JULY 22, 2017 - SOMEWHERE IN OHIO

I was texting a friend recently, making plans to meet up with her in August to go camping, and she wrote, "I can practice my cast iron pot campfire skills."

I responded, "Or we can use my perfectly good propane stove. Or my microwave."

Or my grill.

Or my induction cooktop.

Or my Instant Pot.

Or, now, my new favorite toy, my sous vide precision cooker.

And yes, I do think it's a little silly that I live in a van and carry more cooking devices than outlets to power them. (Not actually true, by the way, *Serenity* has plenty of outlets. But more cooking devices than surface areas to put them on, maybe?)

Certainly more kitchen stuff than room to store it: over the past year, the kitchen and pantry have gradually crept from the obvious space — the cabinets over the stove and the drawers under the microwave — to almost the entire wall of cabinets on the driver's side, plus some room under the bed, plus some room in the space over the cab, plus some floor space, too.

No regrets, though. Last night's dinner was spicy wild sockeye salmon over brown rice with a salad of arugula, avocado, fresh peas, radish, and cucumber with balsamic vinegar.

The salmon was sous vide cooked and tasted incredible. When I was done, I used the warm water from the sous vide pan — completely clean, since the food was cooked in a ziplock bag — to wash the dishes. This morning there was no fish odor, even though I'd had to keep the van closed up during the night because of the rain. Yay!

I wouldn't blame you for thinking, "You're eating sockeye salmon and arugula, no wonder your grocery budget is out of control." But the salmon cost about $3.50/serving, the arugula probably .50, the other ingredients maybe $1.50 combined, which adds up to a cheaper meal than a Chipotle burrito or a McDonald's Big Mac meal.

In other news, I'm in Ohio. It's rainy. I'm starting to wonder if life in Florida and California has skewed my perceptions of how often it's supposed to rain. Maybe the rest of the world really does have rain every day?

Campgrounds in Pennsylvania and Ohio don't seem to include water hook-ups with their electric sites — maybe that's because they think you can just stick a bucket outside and have it fill up overnight? But the grass is green and lush, and it's so hot that the rain feels nice.

Lesson learned this morning, though: if you're enjoying walking in the rain with the hood of your jacket down, perhaps roll the hood up or tuck it inside the coat to prevent it from filling with water? I wouldn't call it an unpleasant surprise, exactly, but when I decided I'd had enough of the rain on my head and pulled my hood up, I splashed myself with all the water that had filled the hood while it was down. Ha.

Last night I read everything I'd written for my current book and decided it was an incoherent mess. Before I gave up on it, though, I wondered if maybe I was just tired. Reread it this morning and yep, I was just tired. Whew.

For many reasons, what I should be doing right now is finding myself a place to sit and write without any distractions — no family or friends to visit, no beaches to roam, no interesting meals to cook.

Actually, "many reasons" boils down to "finances."

But I'm not going to. The aforementioned friend is a single parent with a real job and limited time. I've got a chance to go camping with her and I'm going to take it, which means I'm about to embark on an epic cross-country drive to get to Seattle by early August. Ten days to see the country!

JULY 27, 2017 - BILLINGS, MONTANA

July 25th was the one-year anniversary of the day I said good-bye to my house and hello to life on the road. It started auspiciously enough in a Walmart parking lot in Minnesota.

Yep, my first Walmart parking lot. It was fine. Better than fine, really. I'd spent the night before at a Flying J in Indiana, and although I hadn't slept as horribly as on my first parking lot night, it wasn't exactly relaxing. At the Walmart, I was in a quiet corner, facing a field. I put the window covers up and slept as well as I ever do.

Maybe it was Minnesota, too. While I'm sure Minnesota has its problems, the Walmart had a trash can at every cart rack and no trash visible outside the cans. Go, Minnesota.

That morning, I started off on a relaxed drive out of Minnesota and across South Dakota. I had plenty of time, so I took it slow, pausing at rest stops, reading, writing, checking email.

Unfortunately, it kept getting hotter and hotter and hotter. At one point, my outside temperature gauge read 103. Even with the air-conditioning running full blast, my temperature monitor was sending me constant alerts, because it was over 80 in the van. Both dogs huddled under the AC vents.

Clean, quiet, free, and a nice sunrise, too.

When we got to the Badlands, I paid $20 to enter — my first national park! — and drove slowly through. I'd been thinking I'd camp there for a couple of days at the primitive (i.e., no electricity) campground, but I'd already given up on that idea.

When I drove past the campground with electricity, I gave up on the idea of camping there, too. Even if they had an available site, the campsites were in unrelenting sun.

And it wasn't just the sun — it was windy, with that kind of dry wind that pounds at your ears and makes you immediately want to lick your lips again and again and again. I got out of the van at a scenic overlook to walk the dogs and lasted maybe ninety seconds. If I'd been a pioneer woman in South Dakota, I would have been one of the ones driven crazy by the isolation and the wind. I would have been hallucinating monsters and terrified to leave the house in no time.

So I kept driving. I'd been reading signs for Wall Drug all the way across South Dakota. Either billboards are cheap in South Dakota or Wall Drug has a lot of money to spend on them. Maybe both. But it sounded like kitschy fun, so I decided I'd find a place to stay in Wall and explore the town. Except when we got there, late afternoon, it was still so hot that I couldn't leave the dogs alone in the van.

New plan: Mount Rushmore!

Between stops to feed and walk the dogs and dinner for me, it was after 8 when I arrived. I'm not sure what I expected, but it felt like I'd secretly drifted into a universe where Disney had taken over America. Specifically, the Frontierland version of Disney.

If I had lots of money, a kid to enjoy silly tourist stuff with, and didn't have to worry about the dogs, I could see having fun there. As it was, though, I did a literal drive-by.

I then found a Flying J truck-stop. My third night in a row in a parking lot! But it was by far the worst — busy, crowded, with a casino nearby and a ton of trucks. People wandered by the van until late at night, and I was awake until after midnight, then up at 5:30.

When I woke up, I started driving. I made it out of South Dakota, through a tiny (beautiful!) corner of Wyoming, and into Montana, before discovering that the bathroom floor was sopping wet. I had a fleeting second of wondering if a dog was responsible but it was clean water. Clean water, unfortunately, coming from behind the toilet.

Yeah, a pipe broke.

If it wasn't so damn hot and if I hadn't been driving all day and into the night for days, and if I hadn't slept in parking lots for three nights in a row, I think I'd have the energy to be pissed off about how many things have gone wrong with this tiny house on wheels. I feel like fury and frustration are reasonable responses, but I'm just not feeling them.

It's tedious, but it is what it is.

But it definitely feels like Year Two has started with a whimper, not a bang. Or maybe that should be a splash?

JULY 29, 2017 - SOMEWHERE IN MONTANA

When I decided to do my epic cross-country run, I planned to relax for a couple days in South Dakota — the halfway point — but anticipated the rest of the trip going by in a blur of highways. I was just going to drive until I got to my destination.

The temperatures in South Dakota changed the first half of that plan and the plumbing problems changed the second half. I wound up in Billings, calling RV repair places.

The approved Winnebago dealer, Pierce RV, wanted a $150 priority charge — money for nothing except moving me to the front of their queue — plus $175 an hour after that.

The second couldn't look until August 1.

The third could see me on August 9th, but gave me some other names to call.

The fourth place, Merta RV, said they were really busy, but I could come by at 3 on Thursday and they'd try to squeeze me in.

So there I was in Billings, waiting for a 3 PM appointment. What to do?

On the spur of the moment, I decided to try to take care of the other things *Serenity* needed or would need in the near future: an oil change, her tires rotated, her 20K mile inspection. I stopped by the Dodge dealer to see if they could fit me in. They could, they did.

Done, I decided I might as well go wait in the parking lot at Merta, check my email, maybe even write. The writing didn't happen, because I'd barely been there twenty minutes when the service guy came and took the van away. In no time, he was back, handing me the keys and telling me I was all set. And for less money than the approved dealer wanted just for putting me on their schedule.

From frustration to gratitude, in 24 stressful hours. Thank you, Montana!

JULY 30, 2017 - PHILLIPSBURG, MONTANA

Driving long distances is not my idea of fun. I don't think I'd make a good trucker. But there's a point where you get into the zone and it gets easier and easier to just keep going. Suddenly two hours passes without notice and driving into the night is almost easier than stopping.

Unfortunately, my break in Billings broke me out of the zone. When I got back on the road on Thursday, I lasted barely an hour before I was ready to call it quits.

But I had an idea. In Arkansas, I visited Crater of Diamonds State Park and ever since, I wanted to go sapphire mining in Montana. When I googled, one of the mines was reasonably close to Highway 90.

It would add maybe an hour of extra driving along a scenic highway, plus an hour at the mine, but I thought it would be a nice break and something to look forward to. I figured I'd get there about 2, be back on the road by 3 or maybe 3:30, and then make it to the Montana border before stopping for the night.

But I screwed up. One tiny wrong turn, some minor carelessness with my google research, and I wound up at a store in Phillipsburg instead of the mine I was looking for. The store, however, had a sign that said, "Free camping."

I like signs like that.

It turned out that the mine was about half an hour away and behind the mine were campsites, first come, first served. If there was still room, I could spend the night there.

Done.

The mine was, in fact, not much like Crater of Diamonds. Instead of sitting in the dirt and digging, you buy a bucket of gravel for $25. You get a mesh grate, some big tweezers, and a thing like a test tube with a plastic top with a hole in it. You put some dirt in the grate, rinse it in a wooden trough of water, then dump it out on a table. Carefully, because the sapphires are the heaviest of the rocks, so as you bounce and rock the grate in the water, they should be sinking to the bottom. When you flip the grate, they should be sitting on top of the gravel.

One of the guys working there gave me a demo to get started and when he dumped the grate, a blue stone was sitting on top of the pile, exactly as advertised. It was both delightful and sort of like winning the slot machine on your very first quarter. I wondered whether I was going to spend the next hour feeling like a failure when I didn't find any more.

Nope.

By the time I finished, I'd found 41 tiny sapphires. Every time I dumped the dirt, I found a sapphire. Once I picked one out of the dirt without even rinsing it. I'm not even sure I found all of them, because I was one of the last people there, so I was trying to hurry by the end of my bucket.

Results aren't guaranteed, of course, but they say every bucket has some sapphires in it. Most of them aren't worth processing (heat-treating and faceting), but people do sometimes find larger sapphires, 3 carats or more, that can be worth hundreds of dollars. So there is still that element of playing the lottery, but one where you're guaranteed to win something.

Plus, free camping!

Unfortunately, my anxiety level on Friday evening was prohibitively high.

It was such a beautiful night, but my anxious brain was sure that danger lurked nearby.

I wanted to take a long walk with Zelda — we haven't been getting nearly enough exercise — and I just couldn't.

Bears, rattlesnakes, strangers... I was totally scolding myself, but I was also not leaving the van.

Just not.

The best I could do was about five minutes. It was a beautiful moonrise, an incredible setting, and I took a minute to enjoy the crisp, cold air — and then the smoke from my neighbor's campfire started me worrying about forest fires. Despite being annoyed with myself, I couldn't sleep until I had the van packed and ready to go, in case we needed to run away from fire in the middle of the night.

Sometimes I hate my brain.

On Saturday morning, though, I forced myself to walk Zelda down the road toward the mine. I wasn't going to try to do anything challenging — no wandering into the forest or off on any trails — but I thought I'd walk along the road out to the main road and maybe along it for a while. I'd started to relax and enjoy the beautifully chilly morning when we rounded a curve in the road and a big brown thing lifted its head and looked at us.

Total jump.

And then a relieved laugh. It was a moose.

I've always wondered what Zelda would do if faced with a bear and I think the moose gave me my answer: she would take her cue from me and back cautiously away. She saw it and she was interested, head tilted, ears up, but when she saw that I wasn't going any closer, she followed me away from it without protest.

ON AGORAPHOBIA & ANXIETY

I discovered that I met the clinical criteria for Panic Disorder with Agoraphobia while reading the *DSM-IV: Diagnostic and Statistical Manual of Mental Disorders*. (At the time, I was in graduate school, getting a master's degree in mental health counseling, so it wasn't just light reading.)

I found the discovery annoying.

I already knew I was bipolar (or, in preferred lingo, had bipolar II disorder.) I'd been swinging back and forth between deep depression, including suicidal ideation, and focused, high-achieving productivity, since I was eleven years old. I had a psychiatrist and was on my fifth therapist. It wasn't like I thought I was sane.

Going to five therapists isn't a mark of my mental illness, though: it's a demonstration of my willingness to work on my mental health.

Yet here I was — after years of therapy! — realizing that my reluctance to leave my house, my avoidance of crowds, and my inability to enjoy live music in enclosed spaces were actually diagnosable, not just aspects of my personality.

I could even, without any hesitation, trace those limitations back to specific experiences in my past. The unknown guy who groped me on a dance floor; the stranger who masturbated against me on a bus; the scary dude who followed me and a friend off the New York City subway.

Plus the times I fainted as a young adult: once in a store, once on the subway.

I felt vulnerable in crowds and I hated feeling vulnerable.

Once I realized, though, that I was letting assholes from my past shape my present and my future, I was determined to change.

Alas, that's never quite as easy as saying, "I'm going to be different now."

Most therapists these days practice cognitive behavioral therapy. It focuses on our thinking, trying to help us change our thoughts, attitudes and beliefs. It's great for learning to reframe our experiences.

For example, if something happens — like, say, you discover water pouring through the roof of your brand-new, very expensive camper van — CBT can help you move your thoughts from, "What an absolute fucking nightmare," to "This is a problem with a solution."

But fear is a physical response. Fear is your heart racing, your throat closing. It's feeling like you can't breathe and desperately need to escape. My rational mind often believes I'm being ridiculous when I'm afraid or anxious, but changing my thinking doesn't usually change my feelings.

Instead, I use an approach from a type of therapy called Acceptance and Commitment Therapy (ACT). Instead of trying to change your thoughts, ACT says, "Yep, that's a feeling, embrace it. This is the way you feel. Now move on, what can you DO that will help you feel better?"

Not what will you think, because your thinking isn't the problem, but what action will you take?

In that moment in Montana, packing up the van helped me feel safer. It didn't stop me from being annoyed with myself, however.

AUGUST 23, 2017 - SOMEWHERE IN WASHINGTON

I learned something new about fear today. I wouldn't have thought I had much to learn about fear — it feels like a subject on which I'm an expert.

But I was camping with Seattle friends, P and R. We'd just seen the eclipse and even though we weren't in totality, it was pretty damn cool. It hadn't gotten dark, but the light had definitely changed and there'd been a noticeable drop in temperature.

But it was warming up and the sun was beautifully golden. Nothing like an eclipse for making one appreciate sunshine.

We were climbing a hill, headed to a trail that would take us to a lake. There was no real path, we were just making our way along rocky ground, through scrubby bushes.

Blueberry bushes, in fact.

I'd gotten out in front with the dogs (three of them, all off-leash), probably because they didn't care about blueberries and neither did I. After spending hours this summer picking blueberries in Pennsylvania, discovering the random leftover wild berry wasn't exciting to me.

I turned and looked down the hill. It was so incredibly beautiful — the mountains, the clear sky, the pine trees — that I set Bartleby down and pulled out my phone to take a photo.

And then R straightened up.

In an absolutely casual voice, he said, "Bear."

I waited for him to continue the sentence. Bare what?

And then I followed his gaze, out across the hill in the other direction.

Oh. Right. Bear.

Trying to take a picture of the bear didn't even cross my mind. But this is the photo I took right before we saw the bear.

No, no, I mean, BEAR!

I didn't take a picture. It didn't even occur to me until later.

Instead, I dropped to a crouch and put a hand on Zelda's collar. She, as always, was right next to me. I held out a hand for Bartleby, who, upon the indication that a treat might be in store, trotted over.

I grabbed his collar, too, then realized I didn't have their leashes. P was carrying them.

So I waited.

It felt like a very long time before she made it up the hill, but I'm sure it was about a minute.

I think we were all torn between wanting to watch the bear and wanting to get the hell out of its way. If it had been going in another direction, we probably would have stood there and admired it, just like we'd been admiring the eclipse.

An incredible feat of nature, right?

But since it was trundling toward us — or rather toward the blue-

129

berry bushes we were standing among — getting out of its way seemed like a good idea.

It wasn't until we were moving away that I realized I was maybe a little scared.

I didn't feel scared, but bears don't want to run into us anymore than we want to run into them. A bear would never approach three people and three dogs if it knew we were there.

All we needed to do was make sure it was as aware of us as we were of it, and our encounter would get no closer. In other words, we needed to make noise.

We needed to sing.

But I couldn't remember a single song lyric.

Seriously, not a one. No Girl Scout songs, no hymns, no pop ear worms, nothing. I couldn't even remember the lyrics to that Christmas song with the bells.

In other words, "Jingle Bells."

Yes, I tried and failed to remember, "Jingle bells, jingle bells, jingle all the way."

Total adrenaline brain fog.

Apparently, it's hard to sing when you're scared.

Fortunately, my singing was not required. But we never did make it to the lake.

SEPTEMBER 5, 2017 - ARCATA, CALIFORNIA

I wanted to spend some time exploring Oregon this fall.

Two things happened to change that plan: 1) Oregon, like far too much of the west, started burning down and 2) my friend Suzanne, who lives in Arcata, California, had a week off in early September.

Instead of wandering around Oregon, I drove straight through, with a single, largely sleepless, night at a rest stop, notable only because it was my first night at a highway rest stop and my first chance to discover that rest stops are not peaceful places to spend the night.

It might be my last night at a highway rest stop, too.

I got to Arcata on Friday. It was nothing like I expected. I knew it was a small town. I knew it was remote. I knew it was foggy a lot of the time, with year-round temperatures in the 50s and 60s.

And I guess all of those things are true, but apart from the remote — yes, it was difficult to get to — it was still not what I expected.

It's cute as anything, and not so small. Two bookstores, three theaters, multiple grocery stores and sushi restaurants, art galleries and housewares stores and furniture stores.

Small is relative, but when I think small, I picture Southern small, where a single road has a gas station, a Dollar General, and a donut shop, and that's considered a town. By that standard, Arcata is a city.

On Saturday, Suzanne had to work, so I had a quiet day — much needed after my long drives — hanging out at her house. At lunchtime, though, we met up at the local farmer's market.

It was insanely hot.

I say that as a Floridian.

Insanely hot.

I'd been promised cool weather and fog: instead I got bright sun, 97 degree temperatures, and smoke-filled air. The heat broke records, not just for the day but for the entire time temperatures have been measured here.

I was happy to get back to the relative cool of her house, where all the dogs (her two, my two) lay around and panted, while Greg (Suzanne's husband) and I sat on our computers, every once in a while saying, "Wow, it's hot."

The next morning, we went to the beach with all the dogs. It was glorious. Hot enough that shorts were fine, but with a cool breeze. The dogs were allowed off-leash and three of them ran around like puppies, while even B managed a good long walk and a lot of sniffing at interesting smells.

Z chased sticks and splashed into the water and smiled happy dog smiles. We could have walked forever if we'd left B at home. He was a trouper, though. He probably walked a solid mile, which is a long, long way for a small dog in congestive heart failure.

SEPTEMBER 17, 2017 - SOMEWHERE IN CALIFORNIA

I've been thinking about fear some more. This time it started when I didn't pick up a hitchhiker.

Recently I told a friend the story of the last hitchhiker I ever picked up, about eighteen years ago. It's a long story, but the short version is that I picked him up because it was snowing and I thought he was stranded. I spent the ride letting him believe increasingly elaborate lies as he made me increasingly nervous. When I dropped him off, I drove away feeling lucky that I hadn't wound up a statistic, resolving never to take that chance again.

I've seen a lot of hitchhikers on my way south, none of whom challenged that resolution. Oregon, in particular, had quite a few, but I suspect your average unshaven guy in dirty khaki doesn't expect a solo woman to stop for him and indeed, would be quite surprised if I did.

But the hitchhiker I didn't pick up yesterday was not your average unshaven guy in khaki. He was older, gray-haired, and from his gear, camping. Probably on a long bike trip, and I'm going to guess that something had gone wrong, maybe with his bike, because he was trudging along, walking his bike, head down. I actually drove by him twice, because I took a wrong turn and had to backtrack, and the second time, he, clearly impulsively, stuck out his thumb. I kept driving.

For the next several miles, I alternated between feeling guilty and scolding myself for feeling guilty. I felt guilty because I think he needed help and I could have helped him.

On the other hand, he was only three or four miles away from a town, and although traffic was scarce, it wasn't the middle of the desert. I certainly didn't owe him a ride.

Plus, I really don't want to wind up playing a starring role in a cautionary tale about hitchhikers.

Eventually, though, I started thinking about fear. Rational fear, irrational fear. Fear that stops me, fear that I face.

When I was in Seattle, P described me as bad-ass to one of her friends. I demurred. Nope, not me.

I'm quite cowardly.

I tell myself scary stories all the time. I worry about everything — flat tires, getting lost, coyotes, alligators, bears, corrupt policemen, propane explosions, the end of the world — seriously, everything.

If it is possible to worry about something, I guarantee I have worried about it. Mice carrying hanta virus, stepping on HIV-infected needles, falling off a cliff — I have it covered.

That said, I'm trying to live a life where I don't let those thoughts and feelings stop me.

Yesterday, I stopped at a scenic vista overlooking Mono Lake. I admired the view, then started looking for a place to spend the night. There were plenty of options, but I didn't know how far I wanted to go, where I wanted to stop, what I wanted to do. Decisions, decisions.

There was this place: Fossil Falls, a BLM campground. It sounded interesting. But also remote. Isolated. Potentially... well, scary.

I decided I would drive through and check it out. If I didn't like it, I'd keep driving and maybe spend the night in a Walmart parking lot. It's funny that parking lots have become not-scary — I still remember how freaked out I was my first night in a parking lot, but that was a long time ago.

So Fossil Falls. Well, a picture is worth a thousand words, right?

Definitely remote. Definitely isolated. Definitely, well, scary.

At least if you're me and not the kind of camper who loves remote wilderness and doesn't worry about serial killers and rabid coyotes.

I felt like I could see forever and not see any other human thing. Just mountains and desert. When the sun set, I couldn't see a single light created by a human being except for the ones I'd brought with me.

This morning, B decided he had to go out at 5AM. I complained bitterly, but I got up. It was still dark, but with a sliver of crescent moon and the morning star. It was chilly, but not cold, so I made myself some coffee and sat outside on the van's step to watch the sunrise.

All by ourselves in the desert.

When it got light enough, I took Zelda for a walk. We visited the falls — fossilized because the water is centuries gone, but once upon a time, a river flowed through the volcanic rock. When we got back, I set up my chair and wrote while the sun got higher in the sky and it started to get warm.

I'm so glad that I didn't let fear stop me from staying here.

Of course, that doesn't mean I'm going to start picking up random hitchhikers. It's not irrational to be careful about letting strangers into my home.

But I'm not going to let fear drive my decisions, either. "Once upon a time, something bad might have happened but didn't," shouldn't be a hard-and-fast rule for how I live my life. Neither should, "I heard a scary story about something bad that happened to someone else."

SEPTEMBER 24, 2017 - THE GRAND CANYON, ARIZONA

This morning, Zelda and I hiked from the North Rim Campground, set in a pine forest, to the Grand Canyon Lodge, which overlooks the canyon. I sat on a bench there, Zelda enthusiastically appreciating all the miscellany of smells (in other words, being a totally non-peaceful pain) and admired the view.

When I envisioned the Grand Canyon, I pictured a crowded scenic overlook. Lots of tourists. Dry, sandy air. A big hole in the ground.

Instead, I got a quiet bench, total solitude, the sun rising in the east, storm clouds overhead, a deep chill in the air, a happy dog, a fantastic view, and an unexpectedly intense burst of grief.

I so wanted to call my mom and tell her where I was, what I was looking at. She loved to travel. But she died in 2011 from pancreatic cancer, a quick, brutal illness.

You'd think after six years, I'd be used to the fact that I couldn't call her, and mostly I am. But every once in a while, the grief rolls over me like a wave.

I let it roll.

And when it ebbed, as it always does, I got up and got going. I needed propane, so I did that, then took the dogs on a drive. I stopped at a scenic overlook, looked at the Grand Canyon and was awed all over again.

And then I moved on to the next spot and looked at it again and was a little less awed.

And then I moved on to the next spot and looked again and thought, yep, canyon. Big hole in the ground.

At the next spot, I started looking at the people around me and wondering what their stories were as I glanced at the canyon.

By the time I finished the scenic drive, I was over the canyon. It's spectacular and you have to admire it, but once you've seen it, it's seen.

It was what I expected it to be.

I was feeling sad about that as I returned to the campground. Here's this amazing, incredible spot — truly, one of the wonders of the world — and I'm already jaded about it. I've seen it in so many pictures, read about it in books, viewed it on television. It held no mystery. No wonder.

And then I saw this squirrel. Weirdest squirrel ever.

It was the second time I'd seen it (or its cousin). The first time had been from a distance and I hadn't even been sure it was a squirrel. I thought maybe it was a tiny skunk.

It was black, with a pure white fluffy tail. From up close, it had the funniest ears. Not quite rabbit ears, but big ears, much too big for a squirrel. What the heck?

I couldn't get a picture of it, because Z was with me and the squirrel was not dumb enough to stand still to let Z investigate, so I asked a ranger.

Me: "That squirrel with the white tail, is it some kind of genetic fluke? Part albino? Or do you have special squirrels here?"

He didn't laugh at me, but he did smile.

Yes, they have special squirrels. It's the Kaibab squirrel, found only — only! — at the north rim of the Grand Canyon. If I'd gone to the south rim, I wouldn't have seen it.

R was animal-obsessed when he was little. We watched vast quantities of *Animal Planet*, yet here was an animal I'd never heard of in my own country. In a major tourist destination in my own country.

It brought back every bit of the sense of wonder that I had when I first saw the canyon in the morning light.

SEPTEMBER 24, 2017 - HOMOLOVI RUINS STATE PARK, AZ

Today has been, without a doubt, without even a close contender, the worst day of my journey. I'm not sure I even want to write about it, because I don't feel well enough to believe it's over.

But I'm safely camped at a nice campground, staying here for two nights, plugged into electricity, and it's only 4 PM, so maybe I should be counting my blessings instead of mourning my misery.

I woke up in the night to stomach pain. Indigestive-type stomach pain. At first it wasn't so bad, but it got steadily worse until I was tossing and turning, wondering how I'd given myself food poisoning.

I was listing all my food, trying to think how it could be to blame. Was the pesto too old? Did I not wash the radishes well enough? Was the water in my tank — which I don't drink but did use to wash the vegetables — contaminated?

At various points through my entirely sleepless night, I wondered whether I was dehydrated or having a heart attack, whether it was my gall bladder or a kidney stone, whether I needed an emergency room or should be calling a ranger for help.

I searched my medicine cabinet for something, anything, that would relieve some of the pain and found, unsurprisingly, nothing.

The dogs were as restless as I was. My squirming around kept them on the move. Eventually B wanted to go out — still dark and temperatures in the 20s. I didn't care. I was awake anyway and thought maybe the cold air would help. It didn't.

Then Z wanted to go for her walk. Really wanted it. We'd had a terrific walk yesterday and she loved the cold weather. She was bouncy and energetic and all ready for morning to begin.

I wound up literally snarling at her, because I was face-down, knees to chest, some sort of modified child's pose, trying my best to breathe, and she kept sticking her nose under my arms and trying to lick my face.

Even the sweetest dog understands a snarl; after that she curled up on the dog bed and watched me attentively, trying to decide what I was doing and if I was ever going to take her for a walk.

Answer: no. I wasn't sure I had walking in me.

But I did let her out on a tie-out while I tried to decide what to do. I was pretty sure I had food poisoning. I didn't know how and I was going to have to throw away everything in my fridge because I had no idea what had gone bad, but what else could it be?

And there's no cure for food poisoning. You ride it out and stay hydrated.

Unfortunately, my reservation at the North Rim was over and the campground was full, so I needed to move on.

I did one thing at a time. One item put away, one job done, punctuated with sitting on the floor and rocking. It hurt. It really, seriously, fucking hurt. It felt like my intestines were tying themselves in knots.

Not to be too graphic, but my system had completely cleaned itself out except for copious amounts of gas. Ridiculous amounts of gas. I could have won a belching contest against a world contender, but it only ever alleviated the pain for a moment or two.

And then I realized — the day before, my bag of crackers had inflated. I had to pop it to open it. And the top popped off my plastic container of balsamic vinegar as if expelled by an invisible force.

Gas, in other words.

Could I have altitude sickness? Was the Grand Canyon even high enough for altitude sickness?

Unfortunately, I had no internet to find out. But if my problem was altitude sickness, then I needed to get to a lower elevation.

I started driving. After an hour, I stopped and took a nap, because yes, the pain eased off some. Not entirely. I feel like someone punched me in the stomach a bunch of times and food is still not an option. (I tried. Bad idea.)

And then I kept driving. I wanted to find a decent cell signal so I could look up altitude sickness and elevations of my projected destinations. Also, annoyingly, generator repair, because my generator wouldn't start. I also wanted a pharmacy to get something, anything, that might help me feel better. Plus, no coffee meant a caffeine withdrawal headache, adding to my misery.

Exhausted, aching, nauseous, I kept driving and driving. Watching the odometer. One mile at a time, that's all I needed to do. And then another mile. And then another. I kept checking my cell phone as I drove for a Verizon signal that never showed up.

It was the longest drive through pretty scenery ever.

I wound up driving straight past Flagstaff. At 6900 feet, I could tell from how much it hurt that I wouldn't be sleeping there. I'm now at Homolovi Ruins State Park and it's still a little too high.

At 4900 feet, it's exactly where elevation sickness can start. I think I'd probably be better off a few hundred feet lower. But there's electricity and a cool breeze and hot showers and I was wiped out. I just couldn't keep driving.

I know I should count my blessings: the worst day of my journey did not include an emergency room, a morgue, or the police. It could have been worse. But it still sucks and I still feel miserable and I really wish someone would miraculously show up to deliver some soup and painkillers.

Serenity at Homolovi Ruins.

On the good news front, though, the Facebook *Travato Owners and*

Wannabees group totally came through for me on the generator. Turns out the generator also suffers from altitude sickness, which is fine, because I am never going near a mountain again. (Probably not true. Probably a situational exaggeration.) Ten minutes of reading old posts and I found instructions for how to get it going again.

And now there is a bee buzzing around the van. Seriously, universe? Seriously? But I'm going to go help it find freedom or else mercilessly slay it, ideally without getting stung.

SEPTEMBER 28, 2017 - BLUEWATER, NEW MEXICO

Yesterday, I followed a rather circuitous route to this park, which resulted in me once again turning a three hour drive into a five hour drive. How do I manage to do that so often?

In this case, it turns out that Bluewater State Park has two sides to it and two campgrounds: one is primitive, no hook-ups, and the other has hookups and paved sites.

I went to the primitive side first, not on purpose. I thought about staying once I was there. It was remote and I would have been alone by the side of a lake, which could have been fun.

Except it was raining. Sort of a lot, or at least it felt like a lot.

I didn't want my fun to be "got stuck in wet dirt and couldn't get out" or "got caught in a flash flood and drowned." Sometimes anxiety is irrational and sometimes it's sensible. Heading to the more developed side of the park and camping on top of a hill felt sensible.

Along the way, I passed a Walmart and thought, "Oh, I really need to go there."

And then I thought, "What for?" and kept driving.

Answer: I needed drinkable water, drat it. That means I'll be moving on in the morning because water is not optional.

OCTOBER 10, 2017 - SOMEWHERE IN COLORADO

Zelda and I had a super short morning walk, because it was uncomfortably cold. The degrees didn't look too bad — 46, I think — but the wind had a chill to it that cut straight through my coat.

It was a moving day, so I had to disconnect the water. The hose was stiff and unyielding, and the metal of the connector was so cold it felt like it was burning my hand when I was unscrewing it. It was nowhere close to freezing, but a definite reminder that van life is not compatible with a northern winter.

I've been figuring that out anyway. It's been a while since I whined about dirt, but it's still my least favorite part of van life. The combination of cold weather, limited water, and abysmal campground showers means I've spent a lot of time recently feeling Not Clean. I used to fantasize about baths, but now the combination of a hot shower and clean sheets has almost as much appeal.

OCTOBER 14, 2017 - LAKE OF THREE FIRES, IOWA

On Wednesday, when I was trying to decide where to head next, my priority was, sadly, a shower. Yep, some people look for famous landmarks, beautiful drives, incredible natural wonders, even good restaurants, but me, I just wanted to feel clean again.

Serenity does have a shower, albeit with limited water and drainage. But my mirror broke back in August and I haven't replaced it, and the door of the medicine cabinet is just bare wood. I'm reluctant to let it get wet. Bad enough that I need to replace the mirror; I don't want to have to replace the entire cabinet. Since then, I've only showered when visiting people or in campground showers.

Campground showers are a mixed bag. Some are fine, perfectly reasonable. Some are great. I still remember one in Texas with incredible water pressure and unlimited hot water. It was amazing, despite a few dead bugs in the corners. Those are common to all of them, in my experience.

The ones I've visited lately, though, including the one here, don't

let you control the temperature or the water flow. You push the —
what should it be called, a spigot? A handle? It's a little more than a
button, a lot less than a faucet. But you push the metal thing and
water comes out of the shower head at whatever temperature the park
sets, for an undetermined period of time.

It's not a fun shower.

It's not a fun shower when it's 75 degrees and being wet is
comfortable; it's a decidedly un-fun shower when temperatures are in
the 50s. Campground shower houses don't tend to be heated, after all,
which makes sense — people who are camping in cold weather should
dress appropriately. But it's hard to shower wearing cold weather gear.

Nice big campsites

This is a beautiful place, though. If it weren't for the showers, I could easily see staying here for the entire two weeks one is allowed to stay. Well, if it weren't for the showers and for the inevitability of the fast approaching seasonal change. Winter is coming and I need to get to a warmer climate.

OCTOBER 22, 2017 - SOMEWHERE IN ILLINOIS

I'm losing track of states and places and park names. Fortunately, my photo app had no such problem. It told me I was currently in Wayne Fitzgerrell State Park in Barren, Illinois.

I didn't believe it: who names a town 'Barren'? Doesn't that seem like it's just asking for people to be depressed about living there? So I double-checked with my phone and my phone thinks I'm in Benton, Illinois.

So, yes, not only am I losing track of where I am, my phone and my photos app are equally confused. At least I've figured out that I'm in Illinois.

The reason I wasn't sure is because I left Missouri intending to do laundry, go grocery shopping, then drive across Illinois and Indiana and into Kentucky, which is where I wanted to stop for a few days. But everything took longer than I wanted it to and then, most critically, the rest stop on the highway was closed, and B needed to go.

My choice was to drive another hour to the next rest stop with a whimpering dog at my feet, get off the highway and find a reasonable parking lot with a nice verge of grass, or say the hell with it and find the nearest campground. I went with the latter.

But the campgrounds are all blending together. One after another, a different day, a different set of trees. Sometimes water, sometimes not. Sometimes starry skies, sometimes cloudy mornings. I'm going to have to start coming up with some distinctive event for each campground or they're all just going to be a blur in my memory.

In this campground, the distinctive event would be Zelda, bolting through the screen door to chase an entire herd of deer. She stopped before she went into the woods with them, but I scolded her anyway.

I'm trying to convince the dogs to pretend the screen is actually a door, but they're not buying it. She didn't feel guilty at all.

NOVEMBER 16, 2017 - MERRIT ISLAND, FLORIDA

People keep asking me how much longer I'm going to travel.

It's a legitimate question. I've been wondering myself. But I don't know the answer.

Being back in Florida definitely feels like coming home, more than any other state, which is unexpected. I lived in California and New York for longer than I lived in Florida, and I spent my entire childhood visiting Pennsylvania.

But Florida feels comfortable. Florida feels easy. Sort of.

I almost cried yesterday when the grocery store didn't have the dog food I wanted. It was my grocery store, a home store for me. But I had to hunt for the dog food and then it wasn't there.

Change happens. A grocery store changing brands, re-organizing aisles, that is not the type of change that should make one want to cry.

I think, though, that navigating unfamiliar grocery stores has turned into one of the most exhausting elements of a life of continual travel for me. In my first month on the road I loved the adventure of a new store. Sometimes I still do. Often I still do.

But some days all I want is to get in and get out. I don't want an adventure, I just want to get my need met as quickly as possible so I can get back to whatever I'm doing that is more interesting to me. Yesterday it was to get on the road so that I could come to Merritt Island and write with Lynda. I didn't want to waste hours hunting for the right dog food.

As it happens, I didn't. I bought some strange canned food, ridiculously expensive and radiating organic healthiness, so I could get moving, and today B and I are paying the price. Dogs don't react well to abrupt changes in food.

Poor B. He didn't need an upset tummy on top of the wheezing. He'll be okay, though. I also bought ingredients to make the homemade food he likes, so if I can't find the right food today, he'll get to have chicken and sweet potatoes for dinner and he'll be delighted.

Meanwhile, my travel plans for the next six weeks or so involve nothing new: familiar driveways, a couple of familiar state parks, lots of time spent with people I love.

Florida's also beautiful. I was staying in a friend's driveway, but I took this picture on our morning walk.

At the end of it, after the holidays, I think I'll have a better sense of whether I'm tired of traveling and need to figure out where I can settle down for a while or whether I'm eager to get back on the road. Maybe, like right now, both will appeal.

I read an article titled *The Fear of Missing Out: Or How I Learned to Stop*

Worrying and Love Instagram this morning. It felt beautifully timed, like the universe was reminding me that everyone's life involves trade-offs.

We're all making choices, every day, about what we want to be doing and how we want to do it. No matter what, we're going to miss something.

A while ago, I mostly stopped posting to Instagram because I discovered it was making me feel disconnected. Or fake, maybe?

I didn't like looking at a meal or a view, and thinking about it within a framework of what other people would appreciate about it. A fantastic dinner that wasn't aesthetically pleasing didn't stop being a fantastic dinner, but when I imagined posting the picture, it was with justifications and explanations.

I didn't want to disdain my life because it wasn't attractive enough to share. A photo can't capture the intangibles, anyway — the tastes, the smells, the feelings of community and friendship.

Still, what I liked about Instagram when I first started using it was that it reminded me to appreciate the moment I was in. To celebrate the meal instead of gobbling it, to pause and admire the view instead of glancing out the window and moving on. I might have to try it again.

NOVEMBER 23, 2017 - MOUNT DORA, FLORIDA

In celebration of Thanksgiving, these are the things for which I'm grateful today:

My dogs B is still technically dying, of course, but we all are, really. Ten months after his congestive heart failure diagnosis, he's still ticking along, snuggly and loving and adorable. Admittedly, the last time we were at the vet, I did tell the tech to just muzzle him, because I was pretty sure he wasn't pretending about wanting to bite us. She called it "a party hat" — I called it self-defense. But mostly he is snuggly and loving and adorable.

And Z is terrific. Almost 13 years old, still playing with toys like a puppy. She's losing her hearing, so I'm making special efforts to make sure she's looking at me when I'm telling her how much I adore her, but she's otherwise happy and healthy and a joyful companion.

Clean water Living in a van makes me so aware of my water sources. I finished our "safe" water making coffee this morning. There's some in the tank and it's probably reasonably safe, because I filled it from a clean source just yesterday, but I haven't disinfected the tank since I got the van, so I don't drink out of it.

But I can walk about twenty steps to a source of clean water, and that makes me incredibly lucky. I'm grateful, and very aware of a great many fellow Americans who can't currently say the same, and even more people around the world who can never say the same.

Family and friends I'm so grateful for the times I've had this year with friends and family — from blog acquaintances and writing buddies, to my oldest and dearest friends, to the extended family that I treasure beyond words, and the nuclear family that keeps me anchored when I worry that I'm drifting just a little too much.

Grateful and greedy, I suppose, because I'm looking forward to many more of them. I'm spending Christmas with R, and I'm already making plans for things I want to share with him — movies and television shows, music and food.

Of all the places I've been and the things I've seen and done, I'm most grateful to have spent so much time with the people I care about.

7

2018 - SORROW TO CELEBRATION TO SORROW

FEBRUARY 5, 2018 - CASSELBERRY, FLORIDA

I called the vet at 7:07 AM this morning and much to my surprise, someone answered. Remarkably cheerfully, too, considering how early it was. He told me the vet would be in at 9.

By 9:05, maybe even earlier, Bartleby was in the back on oxygen and an IV. Oxygen is quite expensive considering how readily available you'd think it would be. By 9:15, they'd upped the time they thought he'd need to be on it from an hour (billed in 15-minute increments) to an open-ended, "Let's see how it goes," also adding a slew of other charges to his bill.

I don't even care.

I really thought I was going to be all grown-up and responsible about the economics of having a dying dog and an uncertain income, but nope. If they said, "It's going to cost $1000 and give him another month of good life," I'd hand them my credit card without another word.

Emphasis on the good life, though. Another month where he struggles to breathe and turns away from his food will break my heart on an hourly basis.

And, of course, they really can't know what that $1000 would buy and neither can I. But two days ago, B was still wagging his tail and kissing my face, and last night, he was willing to gobble down some chicken even if his regular food didn't interest him, so today, it's oxygen and x-rays and medication and whatever dollars it takes to give me a chance of some more snuggles and tail wags.

The other day I looked up the difference between worry and fear. It sounds like something I should know, right? It sounds like the difference ought to be obvious. But I wasn't sure it was.

Because I'm not worried — I already know the outcome, how can I worry about something that is inevitable? — but I am afraid. Afraid that I will make the wrong choices, that he will suffer more than he should or live less than he should. The internet let me know that fear is involuntary, but worry is a choice.

So I am choosing not to worry, to trust that I will make the right decisions, that I will know what to do when the time comes. But I am still afraid.

And very, very sad.

FEBRUARY 6, 2018 - CASSELBERRY, FLORIDA

I hate the euphemisms — put down, put to sleep, even euthanize. The reality was, I would have stayed forever with his warm head cuddled against my shoulder, stroking his soft fur, whispering love into his goofy ears. But he was slowly suffocating, fighting the fluid that was filling his lungs and heart, and I couldn't bring myself to be so cruel. So I let him go.

Helped him go.

When the vet was injecting him with the sedative, I was stroking him and telling him what a good dog he was and then I stopped myself and I told him the truth.

"Actually, B," I said, "You peed in places you shouldn't, and sometimes you snapped and snarled at people, and you were very stubborn about refusing to learn any commands, even the easy ones. So I'm not sure I can say you were a good dog exactly. But you were very good at loving me."

I think that's probably the only skill a good dog really needs.

Yesterday was the sixth anniversary of my best friend's death. As his gasping breaths finally slowed down, I told B to find Michelle and take her to a beach. I would like to think that they are there right now, and that B's knees don't hurt and he doesn't get tired after three minutes of running and he isn't scared to play with toys and sticks. And if he wants to go swimming, that she has a warm towel waiting for him.

I will miss him so. I already do.

At Gunter Hill, in Alabama

FEBRUARY 20, 2018 - SOMEWHERE IN FLORIDA

I've realized a couple things about my next few months.

The first is that without B, I don't have such an imperative need to get out of Florida. He was miserable when it was too hot. Even without the congestive heart failure, he was a pudgy little guy with a thick coat of black fur, and the heat was hard on him. Even in 70 degree weather, he'd be panting.

Zelda — white dog, thinner coat, skinny and energetic — doesn't mind the heat nearly as much. And one of the big issues about the heat was that I needed to leave B in the van while I walked Zelda, so I always needed to be able to have the AC running. That's no longer a problem.

I wish it was. I'd much rather be worrying about B and trying to make him comfortable than living without him. But it is what it is.

The second thing isn't a realization as much as it is a hard look at my timeline: I need to be in Florida in May for R's graduation. That gives me two months. And I don't want to spend them driving. Long driving days are exhausting and time-consuming.

There are places I wanted to go — I'd rather be spending spring in the northeast than the south — but I don't want to rush around, spending hours on the road and worrying about getting to my destinations on a schedule that doesn't give me enough time to enjoy them (and to write a book along the way.)

So my current plan, such as it is, is to relax and enjoy the south. I'll have a few more weeks in Florida and then I'll do some exploring in Georgia and maybe South Carolina, maybe even back to Arkansas, and then I'll swing back into Florida for the first part of May. And then May 20th or so, I'll head north, taking my time about it.

After a stressful couple of weeks, I'm relaxing and enjoying my day today. I'm in Lake Griffin State Park, which is a place I've stayed before, but I like it more every time I'm here. It's a small park, close enough to a busy road that you never stop hearing road noise, but I don't mind that.

This morning I took Zelda on a walk down a path that we've never gone on before. I could hear the traffic, but being surrounded by nature, breathing fresh air, seeing greenery and giant palmettos and pretty yellow flowers scattered across dead brown leaves on the ground made me feel like I'd discovered a primeval swamp in the backyard of a strip mall.

Then we reached a spot where the mud was thick and black and goopy and Zelda decided she wanted no part of it. She dragged me back the way we came. Now I'm sitting in the van, windows open, listening to traffic but also birds and breezes in the leaves and a far distant barking dog, and watching a yellow butterfly. It's a beautiful day for writing many words.

MARCH 2, 2018 - SOMEWHERE IN FLORIDA

My friend A asked me last week whether I'd had a dry day yet. I looked at her, puzzled, and she said, "Tears?"

Ah.

The answer was "No."

Losing a dog is unlike any loss I've ever had. It's not more painful — I lost my mom and my best friend, Michelle, in the same miserable six month period, and there were times I wondered if I'd ever stop crying. But missing Bartleby is so constant, such an ever-present emptiness.

I do fine when I'm with other people. I have no trouble making conversation, going places, interacting, even being cheerful. But when Z and I are alone in the van... it's just so quiet without Bartleby.

I want to remember all the good things of the past few weeks: conversations with friends, nice driveways, a fantastic summer roll dinner with Christina, writing with J and A, visiting R in Sarasota and eating dinner outside with Zelda sleeping under the table.

But the truth is that I'm spending a lot of my time feeling over-whelmed by the sad.

MARCH 5, 2018 - SOMEWHERE IN FLORIDA

I was joking with Tim over text about every day being New Year's Day. It's not just that all my resolutions have gone nowhere — did I even make any resolutions? — it's that 2018 is slipping away while I feel increasingly stuck, grinding my gears deeper and deeper into the mud.

The mud is obviously metaphorical, but I'm not even sure what it is.

Depression? Maybe.

Grief, sure.

Lack of productivity leading to self-loathing leading to inertia leading to the dirty dishes piling up in the sink and a blue hair tie sitting in the middle of the floor day after day after day. Why don't I just pick up the damn blue hair tie?

I don't know. It seems like too much work? It's an interesting dash of color in the gray? It reminds me that I should brush my hair? Not that I do, I just think, "Hmm, maybe I should brush my hair," and then I start browsing the internet again.

Today I picked up the blue hair tie. And I washed the dishes and put them away.

Today is the first day of the rest of my life, cliché as that statement is, and if it was the last day I would want to know that I'd used it wisely.

Which means not browsing the internet for hours, not reading books I don't care about, not playing mindless internet games, but yes, taking good walks with Zelda, yes, eating healthy food, and yes, writing some of my own words. And yes, making sure my tiny house is comfortable and cozy and clean.

Time to get started.

MARCH 12, 2018 - SANFORD, FLORIDA

I saw manatees this week.

At least, I think they were manatees. They were big gray lumps, breaking through the surface of the water and then disappearing again.

Too big to be otters, which was my first thought. Too inland to be dolphins or whales, which would have been my second, if I'd been at the ocean.

I wasn't at the ocean. I was actually at a lake whose name I don't know, but which is down the street from a driveway that's been a regular campsite for me.

It made me think about magic. And adventure. And the difference between them.

But also, more importantly, about remembering that magic is right around the corner, all the time, if we just look for it.

MARCH 16, 2018 - REED BINGHAM STATE PARK, GEORGIA

Zelda and I went on a three mile hike today, through pine scrub forests and wetlands, along a boardwalk and a bumpy, tree-root-filled dirt path. And some paved road, too. It was glorious.

It was not, however, our usual first thing in the morning walk, because it was cold at 7AM and it was also crazily dark.

Sunrise was at 7:44 AM, which I know because I asked Alexa. That's actually a solid 32 minutes later than sunrise wherever Alexa thinks I live, which I know because while I was staring out my window at the barely lightening sky, we had this conversation.

Me: Alexa, what time is it?

Alexa: It's 7:08 AM.

Me: Alexa, what time is sunrise?

Alexa: Sunrise is at 7:12 AM.

Me: So why is it so dark outside?

Alexa: ...

Me: Alexa, why is it so dark outside?

Alexa: Sorry, I'm not sure.

Me: Alexa, what time is sunrise in Adel, Georgia?

Alexa: Sunrise is at 7:44 AM.

Me: Wow, that's weird.

Alexa: ...

She's not always the best conversationalist. Still, it's pretty cool that from the comfort of my bed, while buried under my covers — two blankets last night for the first time in months! — I can find out what's happening with the sky.

Anyway, Z and I wound up taking a quick walk, then coming back to *Serenity* for breakfast and miscellaneous chores. Well, I did miscellaneous chores. Zelda had a nap.

But around lunch time we went for our walk and it was spectacular. Probably about fifty-five degrees, with spring popping up around every corner: pink flowers and yellow flowers, but also just the early green leaves starting on bare branches.

I'm happy to be on the road again. My last couple of weeks in Florida were great. I got to spend time with lots of friends, and finished it off with a couple fun days with family. Movies and interesting food and writing with friends, some great conversations and coffee dates — what more could anyone want?

But apparently I also want nature and bird song and for the van to be connected to a safe water supply.

And long walks through interesting terrain, the smell of my neighbors' campfires, and starry, starry night skies.

MARCH 20, 2018 - CLOUDLAND CANYON STATE PARK, GEORGIA

I picked my current campground based on its pretty name. When I read it, I envisioned a land of fluffy white clouds, pristine blue sky, some sort of magical hopping from cloud to cloud over deep ravines, probably birds in primary colors. You know, the anime version of Cloudland Canyon.

Duh.

I should have been picturing fog. Dense, heavy, impressive fog. A Land of Clouds.

Worst fog I've ever driven through, too. I spent a solid ten minutes in almost total white-out debating whether it would be worse to be rear-ended because I was driving too slowly or rear-end someone else because I was driving too fast. I was going at least twenty miles under the speed limit at the time, so I guess that indicates which I chose. But I did think I might still be driving too fast.

I think white-out refers to blizzards, actually. Gray-out? What's the word for when visibility is almost nil in fog?

The stairs into the canyon, with the clouds below us.

MARCH 25, 2018 - SOMEWHERE IN TENNESSEE

I woke up to the sound of Canadian geese complaining. Then I spent the next several minutes sleepily castigating myself for negatively anthropomorphizing birds. Surely they were honking or calling or murmuring.

Then I woke up a little more and realized it was still the middle of the night and those birds were definitely complaining. Not sure what they were complaining about — a raccoon disturbing their slumber, maybe? But they stopped and I went back to sleep and eventually, when I woke up again, their noises were much more like daybreak murmurings.

I'm in Tennessee, currently at a Thousand Trails campground. Yesterday I was remembering the last time I was in Tennessee.

I thought then that the state would probably be beautiful in about two more weeks, but at that moment it was bleak, the trees ugly spires of bare trunk with dead, hanging leaves that should have dropped months ago. I then looked up the date I was last here: coincidentally, but not surprisingly, March 24th. The exact same day.

And yeah, I think Tennessee will probably be nice in two more weeks, but today, it is the epitome of March showers. Overcast, mildly foggy, everything looking gray. Not pretty, but lovely in a Goth sort of way. The kind of lonely beauty that makes cups of tea seem highly desirable.

I was planning on spending more time in Tennessee, but I think instead, I'm going to drift my way south. Or maybe west. But first things first: Z wants her walk.

LATER AT TRACE STATE PARK, MISSISSIPPI

I walked Zelda, got back to the van, and instead of making myself some coffee and starting to write, I packed up and got on the road.

The campground was probably a nice place. But it's the kind where people have annual memberships and leave their trailers at their sites year round.

Stuff accumulates outside the trailers.

Not necessarily bad stuff: potted plants and lights and chairs, golf carts and grills, holiday decorations and signs. But time and weather and entropy quickly combine to turn pleasant vacation gear into shabby, run-down debris.

It didn't just feel like a trailer park, it felt like an abandoned trailer park. Half depressing and half spooky. (The bathrooms, however, were excellent — clean and shiny new.)

A year ago, I would have stayed. I would have stuck it out for the three days of my reservation, feeling like a reservation was a commitment, that because I'd made a plan, I needed to stick to the plan. Now I know better.

One of the best parts of life in a van is moving on when what you've got isn't what you want.

So I got on the road and headed south, along the Natchez Trace. It's a scenic highway along what was once a trail used by bison, Native Americans, and early settlers. At 8 AM on a Sunday morning, I was alone on it and it was gorgeous. I took a couple breaks along the way, went to a grocery store in Tupelo, Mississippi, and then found myself a campsite at Trace State Park.

I picked the park based on the fact that I generally like state parks, that I didn't want to keep driving, and that the sun was showing through the clouds when I walked out of the grocery store. Even though the sky has clouded up again, I feel much happier here. The lake is currently gone — undergoing renovations apparently — so my waterfront spot is a "looking out onto a grassy pit" spot, but it is peaceful and quiet.

I remember sitting in a campground in Louisiana and realizing that there are places where those noisy birdsong relaxation meditations that sound so fake are actually real. This is one of them. If it weren't for the hum of the computer, the only sound would be birds chirping and squeaking and whirring and making all those different mysterious sounds they make. Not complaining, though. They sound quite happy. (But I could be anthropomorphizing. Or maybe that should be projecting.)

MARCH 31, 2018 - LAKE CHICOT, ARKANSAS

Yesterday morning, after many days of rain, the sun rose into a clear blue sky. The temperature was about 50 degrees, so it was chilly, but spring was exploding all over the place.

All the trees are shooting out leaves, so fast they look different from one day to the next, but they're still in the stage where the leaves are tiny and elegant and beautiful. Feathery fragile leaves, instead of an indistinguishable mass of green.

Serenity's campsite at Lake Chicot.

I took Z for a walk and we finally found the nature trail. For obvious reasons (rain, rain, more rain), I hadn't looked for it too hard earlier, but it was such a beautiful day that we kept walking until we found it.

Of course, I shouldn't have been surprised to discover that it was mud central. The whole point of a nature trail is dirt and all the dirt in

this campground is sopping wet. Despite the mud, we started down
the trail, into the woods, but within fifty steps, I knew we wouldn't be
going much farther.

White dog, black mud, limited access to water and laundry
machines — I wanted to explore but I didn't want to spend the next
hour trying to get Z clean before she jumped onto the bed.

I was just about to turn around when we startled a herd of white-
tailed deer. Not a huge herd — maybe six of them? Maybe eight?

They went bounding off through the trees, splashing through
puddles, toward the east, into the rising sun, with the light reflecting
off the water and green all around them.

It was so beautiful that it was unreal. It was like a scene in a movie
that you know has been filtered and faked and never really existed like
that. Except there it was, existing like that, so incredibly purely
gorgeous I just stood in the mud and blinked.

I thought of trying to take a picture, but a photo wouldn't have
captured the chill in the air and the bird sounds surrounding us and
the smells of spring and the movement of the deer, and even the way
my heart was pounding from the surprise of discovering we weren't
totally alone in our little wilderness.

Later in the day, I met a kid in the road. I use the term "met"
loosely. I passed a kid in the road. I smiled and nodded and said, "Hi,"
and he smiled back at me and said, "I like your dog."

I wanted to clap my hand over my heart and swoon and say, "Yes!"
The kids who said, "I like your dog," were one of my favorite parts of
Arkansas last year. I'm so glad that's a thing here. I find them so
endearing.

APRIL 9, 2018 - TOAD SUCK, ARKANSAS

Every once in a while I get into a conversation with someone where
the longer we speak, the more I sense them becoming convinced that
I'm kind of a flake. Not in the special-snowflake sense, but in the...
hmm. You know, some internet research has now convinced me that
"flake" is the wrong word.

Eccentric is much closer to what I mean. It's not that I think they begin to believe me unreliable or selfish or scatterbrained, more that I can see the confusion growing in their eyes. In today's example, it was a conversation about my reasons for being here.

I'm not here because I'm on my way somewhere.

I'm not here because I have family in the area.

I'm not here because I'm a hiker or a biker or a water sports enthusiast.

Nope, it's just because the place has a really good name: Toad Suck

I think that's a perfectly sensible reason to visit a place, but the nice older gentleman I was speaking with found it mystifying, I believe.

The trees at Toad Suck had the light green leaves of early spring.

Fortunately for me, it's also a great campground. I have an extremely nice spot, right on the river, facing the water.

My usual routine when I get to a new campground is to plug in to the electricity and connect to the water if I have hook-ups, then putter around the van. I check my internet connection, look at my email, see what kind of music I can find, get out some things that I put away for travel but are pleasant to have accessible, like my essential oil diffuser and my induction cooktop. Maybe I rest for a while from my drive, maybe I take Z for a walk.

At Toad Suck, I immediately got out my chair and set it up under the tree at my campsite, then sat and admired the river while Zelda tried to sniff every blade of grass. I'm hoping this is going to be a good place to get some writing done.

Also, hoping, I have to admit, for some steady sunshine and warmer temperatures. The more time I spend outside Florida, the more I realize it's called the Sunshine State for a reason and that I have been profoundly spoiled by living there for so long.

Also, that I like sunshine.

The more cold days I spend in the van — not cool days, but days where the temps go below 35, so cold days — the more I know the van is not a cold-weather lifestyle, at least not for me.

APRIL 16, 2018 - EUREKA SPRINGS, ARKANSAS

27 degrees.

27 DEGREES!

Yesterday, I was walking Z, bundled up in leggings and long socks and blue jeans, with a long-sleeved shirt, two hooded sweatshirts, and my windbreaker, my gloves and scarf, and white flakes were falling out of the sky on me.

It was April 15th.

I feel that's simply crazy. I would like to speak to the weather police and report Arkansas.

However, my campground is terrific. It's on an island in the middle of a beautiful lake. It takes approximately 700 steps to do a full loop of the campground, so our exercise is going to be walking in circles. Cold circles.

But the view can't be beat.

Water on all sides meant incredibly beautiful sunrises and sunsets.

APRIL 23, 2018 - SOMEWHERE IN ARKANSAS

On Saturday, I texted my friend Lynda and said, "This illness has moved incredibly quickly from 'maybe I'm sick,' to 'Death is inevitable and I can only hope it comes quickly.'"

Yesterday, R called. I said, "Hello," and he said, "Oh, you don't sound good."

I said, "Yeah, I thought about calling you earlier, but all I really have to say is 'whine, whine, whine.' And now I'm done. How are you?"

So yeah. Whine, whine, whine.

Being sick in a van sucks and I would truly like a real bed, a hot bath, some good drugs — Dayquil would be nice — and another box or two of tissues. And some chicken soup.

Zelda would like someone to take her for a walk.

It is oddly peaceful, though.

In a house, when I'm sick, I'm always in search of something to help me feel better. The hot bath or a more comfortable pillow, a distraction or a drink. I turn on the television, turn it off again. Pick up a book, put it down again. Walk to the kitchen, go back to the bedroom. Try out the couch for a while, then move to the recliner. It's a fretful search for comfort.

In the van, there's nothing I can do, except stare out the window and wait to feel better.

So that's what I'm doing. Waiting to feel better. Fingers crossed that it's sooner rather than later.

APRIL 26, 2018 - AUX ARC, ARKANSAS

I wonder how I'm going to remember places. And then I wonder whether it really matters. I'd like to live so mindfully that my present is always more of my focus than my past, that instead of trying to remember where I was at whatever date of some year gone by, I'm always appreciating where I am.

That said, Aux Arc is the sound of trains rumbling by and Canadian geese murmuring.

MAY 1, 2018 - ON THE ROAD

I spent last Thursday wavering with indecision. I'd intended to go to a meet-up of fellow Travato owners in Jasper and I'd been looking forward to it. It was, in fact, a big part of the reason I decided to spend my month in Arkansas, rather than North Carolina or Georgia.

But I felt like crap. Not so debilitated I wasn't even leaving the van — Zelda was getting her walks again — but taking a shower still seemed like a monumental endeavor, possibly beyond my energy level.

Meeting people, going out to eat, listening to music, canoeing on the Buffalo river, sharing a potluck dinner, all sounded nice, but completely overwhelming. I was still in crawl-under-the-covers and stare-out-the-window mode. And I knew the 16-hour drive to Florida wasn't going to be a breeze.

Zelda made my decision for me on Friday morning. It was a chilly morning, so I was buried in my sheets, tucked up under my warmest blanket. She was snuggled into me so sweetly, curled up in the curve of my back. It was so cozy and nice.

And then it was not cozy and not nice, because there was warm liquid on my back and my sheets and my blankets, rapidly turning cold in the chill of the van. She stood up and gave me a look of puzzled reproach, then moved over to other side of the bed and curled up and went back to sleep.

I did not go back to sleep. Ugh.

This was not the first time this had happened. It might have been the third within a few weeks? But she honestly doesn't seem to have any awareness that she's peeing. She's not showing signs of distress ahead of time, not telling me she needs to go out, not even squatting. She was lying down, and then she was lying down in a puddle of dog pee.

And so was I.

Ugh, double-ugh, triple-ugh.

Adding laundry and a need for clean sheets and a dog with incontinence issues to my trip dropped a heavy weight on the "go home now" side of the indecision teeter-totter. Instead of packing to head north, I called the vet and made an appointment for Z, posted my apologies to the Facebook group and started on the road east.

I didn't leave too early and I didn't push too hard on the drive. I took it reasonably easy, giving myself breaks when I got tired and spending time at rest stops and in grocery store parking lots. I wound up spending the night in a Walmart parking lot. It was a typical parking lot experience, too noisy during the evening, eerily quiet in the early hours of the morning.

When I look at a drive on Google maps and see that it's 16 hours, I subconsciously believe it's going to take me 16 hours of driving time. My conscious mind knows better. That 16 hours doesn't include getting off the highway for gas, the extra driving time to find a place to stay, breaks at rest stops for meals and dog walks, traffic delays and getting trapped behind school buses.

That 16 hours is the totally optimistic, ideal world, robot-chauffeur drive time. Reality is never so quick.

But leaving Arkansas early meant I had plenty of time to get to Florida. Instead of driving all day and staying in another parking lot overnight, I decided to find a campground in the early afternoon and enjoy a tranquil night.

I picked one not quite at random. I didn't want to stay somewhere I'd already been, which ruled out many of the campgrounds on my most direct path home. Also, I really like the Army Corps of Engineers campgrounds. All other things being equal, I'd rather try an unfamiliar ACoE campground than any other option. So I spent a while at my morning rest stop browsing camping options, and eventually picked Cotton Hill Campground.

I got there around 2 and they only had a few spots left, but a two-night minimum stay. First time I'd encountered that, but I didn't hesitate. I was already sick of driving and taking an extra day as a break sounded just fine to me.

ON TYPES OF CAMPGROUNDS

No matter how much research you do and how many reviews you read, every unfamiliar campground is a jump into the unknown.

You might find an awesome campground, but have a horrible site. I stayed at a great campground on the Blue Ridge Parkway where my site was directly across from the dump station. Within easy smelling distance, in fact. I left early.

I stayed at another in New Mexico where the camp host told me I'd picked the worst site in the park, but it had a great view and it worked for me.

Generalizing about campgrounds isn't easy and many people write reviews with opinions based on the experience they had — the lousy neighbors, the bad weather, the rude host — rather than the campground as it might be for you.

That said, here are my thoughts about campgrounds by type:

National Forest campgrounds are my favorites. They don't usually have hook-ups, so you're paying for dry camping, which deterred me from trying them initially, but they tend to be peaceful and beautiful. Reviews often complain about sites not being big enough and roads being challenging, but that's more relevant for people driving big RVs than it is for someone in a camper van.

Army Corps of Engineers campgrounds are often adjacent to dams and reservoirs. They generally seem to prioritize scenic views and reasonable space rather than packing people in. They don't tend to have the amenities of independent campgrounds and some of them are fairly run-down — no fancy showers! — but they're economical, as well as beautiful. They're second on my list.

State Park campgrounds depend on the state. I'd say not all states are created equal, but actually not all states make the same choices. Some states have wonderful systems. Florida is a total winner with some incredibly beautiful state parks. Unless I've already had a bad experience in a state park (ahem, California), state campgrounds are third on my list of campgrounds to try.

National Park campgrounds, in my experience, are incredibly crowded. They're generally well maintained and clean, but they're packed with people, and not just people, but people on the move. They're busy, busy places.

County Park campgrounds are completely erratic. You've got no idea what you're getting when you try a county campground: it might be beautiful or it might be a parking lot for transients.

Harvest Hosts is a membership that gives you access to free camping at wineries, farms, museums, golf courses, and similar locations. You're expected to support the location by shopping with them, but there are no other fees. For me, camping at these sites feels like destination camping: it can be wonderful if you want to go to the winery or museum, but otherwise, you're driving out of your way for a single night stay. Plus, you have to call ahead to arrange your visit with the location and call again on the day of arrival, and that's not always convenient.

Bureau of Land Management campgrounds (or camping), in my experience, are a complete crapshoot. They can be wonderful, they can be horrible. Fees vary, amenities vary, access varies. Do your research or take your chances. Many full-time RVers spend a lot of time on BLM land in the southwest and rave about BLM camping. But on my personal list of harrowing drives — the "oh, shit, this was a bad idea," type of drive — two of the top three spots go to BLM campgrounds in California.

Independent campgrounds, generally speaking, are for a different audience than me. Maybe they're resorts, maybe they're trailer parks, but they typically prioritize paved parking spots and amenities for vacationers or retirees. Some of them are nice, of course, but you pay for what you get.

As I mentioned earlier, you can buy memberships in various organizations for specific independents: KOA, Thousand Trails, Passport America, Good Sam Club, probably others. These vary in quality. In my experience, KOAs are always nice and always expensive; Good Sam Club is pretty reliable; and the others are a mixed bag.

The most expensive places I've stayed were independent campgrounds and while I can certainly think of a couple off the top of my head that were worth the money, I rarely try them these days. I only look at independent campgrounds if I've ruled out all my other options or if someone I trust has recommended the campground. (Or if I have some other reason to be there, such as it being the only campground open during a pandemic.)

That said, almost all of the other types of campgrounds have limits on the length of your stay. If you're looking for a place where you can settle down for a few months, an independent campground is probably your only choice.

MAY 2, 2018 - COTTON HILL CAMPGROUND, GEORGIA

Cotton Hill was fantastic, a beautiful campground at a beautiful time of year.

I had a water hook-up and empty tanks, plus knew I could dump the tanks the next day, so I was profligate with my water use, washing my dishes in hot water and rinsing them thoroughly, and then washing some dishes I hadn't used, but that couldn't hurt to be a bit cleaner. Back when I owned a dishwasher, I never knew how satisfying truly clean dishes could be.

I read books I'd read before, I sat in my outside chair in the sun, I snuggled Zelda when she allowed it, and I took a couple mellow walks.

And I appreciated the air and the birdsong and the water view and my life.

It's so easy for days to blend together — even when they're good days, even when I like them. One good day follows the next and the highlight is a good meal that's a lot like some other good meal from a week earlier, and I remember to be grateful, but I don't remember to savor the moment I'm in.

I forget to breathe and return to worry.

But after two long days of driving and with more driving ahead of me, a peaceful day in a beautiful place where my biggest ambition was to talk Zelda into eating some dog food was golden.

MAY 7, 2018 - SANFORD, FLORIDA

On Thursday, I got nothing done. Zelda had a vet appointment at 4 PM and I spent the day trying to drown my worry in puttering. Laundry, re-organizing cupboards, washing dishes, wiping down the floor, folding clothes in different ways...

Eventually, we made it to the vet, who ruled out a urinary tract infection or kidney problems. That left, as I had suspected, hormone-related urinary incontinence.

Or dementia.

Don't ever google canine dementia.

It's not something you want to know anything about if you love a dog, not unless you're forced to.

Zelda started the incontinence medication on Friday morning. It takes between 5-10 days to take effect, so the fact that she's peed in the van multiple times since then does not mean she's got dementia.

But the incontinence is getting dramatically worse. She went from an unexpected accident inside in February to peeing on my bed on April 13th, to doing it again a week later, then three times within a week, then yesterday three times within the day.

I am... well, somewhat distraught, actually. It's not just the peeing, although that's obviously uncool. Yesterday she managed to pee on two fitted sheets, two pillowcases, and a top sheet. Plus the floor, plus a rug, or maybe two rugs. Fortunately, I'm parked in a friend's driveway, so there's a washing machine nearby.

But she's also not eating well; she's doing weird things like burying bits of food around the van (so not okay); she's sleeping on the floor instead of my bed; and, of course, every odd thing she does now looks like a symptom of dementia to me.

I don't think I could possibly be living a worse lifestyle for a dog with dementia.

After I lost Bartleby, I realized I needed to develop a Zelda Loss Survival Plan. I knew that if losing B was bad, losing Z was going to be devastating.

I loved B, still do, but he was a dog, and I was not his person. He tolerated me at first, loved me eventually, I believe, but I'm not sure the trauma of his early life even made it possible for him to have a person the way some dogs do.

But I am Zelda's person.

I am the center of her universe.

And she's my companion, my buddy, my best friend. My girl. A constant presence in my life for over thirteen years, always at my heels, always my first interaction in the morning, the last at night.

She's been with me through all of the challenges, all the losses of the past ten years. This dog has licked away my tears at least a hundred times. (And if you think that's gross, you probably haven't had as many reasons to cry as I have.) She's been an unwavering, unconditional, boundless source of love.

When I was walking her this morning, I realized that the fundamental problem with my ZLSP is that it also needs to be a LZSP, a Losing Zelda Survival Plan. If her loss isn't a lightning bolt, but a long, slow nightmare that includes her becoming aggressive and no longer recognizing me, I need a different plan.

I have no idea what that plan looks like, but it probably starts with a deep breath.

In this moment, it's a beautiful day in Florida. It's probably going to get too hot, as always, but right now, my window is open, there's a cool breeze, and I'm listening to the neighbor's clucking chickens and some chirping birds.

I will appreciate where I am, I will accept what I'm feeling, and I will not, not, not anticipate the future.

MAY 23, 2018 - MOUNT DORA, FLORIDA

This morning, I knelt on the floor at my dad's house to rub noses with his dog, Gizmo. Gizmo is, I think, a mix of cocker spaniel and poodle*
— golden, soft, fluffy, with an extremely endearing underbite, and a passionate devotion to his person, my dad. With his person out of the room, he was willing to come be loved up by me and maybe even play a little.

When Zelda saw what we were doing, she decided to come play, too. Within minutes, she and Giz were both chasing after a squeaky skunk, racing down the hallway after it, shoving one another out of the way, even playing tug as they were bringing it back to me.

Zelda was play bowing, batting at the toy with her paws, even mock growling, and Giz's tail was wagging a hundred beats a minute.

If I had a tail, it would have been wagging even faster than Giz's.

Sunday before last, Z was sick and getting sicker. Not eating, hiding under the table, lethargic, no energy. Not even interested in going for walks. I'd been bracing myself for the worst and it felt like the worst was coming faster than I could have imagined.

Last Monday, I decided to stop the medication she was on. On Thursday, I got the news that she had no sign of a UTI, so I also stopped the antibiotic she was on. She started getting better immediately.

Yesterday, at my dad's suggestion, I took her to his vet. Instead of recommending an ultrasound and x-rays, which was the next step with Banfield, his vet gave her estrogen.

Wow. Just wow, wow, wow, wow.

The vet said it would take a couple weeks before we'd know whether it was going to help with the peeing problem, but watching her play with Gizmo; having her almost drag me out of the van to go for a walk in the rain; seeing her lick every last speck of food out of her dinner bowl, then nose me and look expectantly for more... I'll buy stock in doggie diapers, I'll plan on doing laundry as often as it takes, but oh, it's so nice to have my girl back!

In other news, R's graduation was lovely. New College students treat commencement as a combination costume party and picnic. It took place at sunset, by the water, and while there were appropriate speeches, suggestions to go out and change the world, and professors attired with dignity in their academic robes, the students were celebrating.

R had been torn earlier in the day whether he was going costume-party or dignity, but he went with the costume and I got to watch —

with immense pride and much cheering and clapping — my beloved son accept his diploma while dressed as a lobster.

I'd been worried that I might cry, but I think it's actually impossible to cry when watching a lobster graduate from college. There was much beaming with pride, though.

edited to add a message received via email: The Giz is pissed at you. He is not in any way genetically related to any Cocker Spaniel. He is a ferocious peek-a-poo, a descendent of a fierce line of savage Pekingese who mauled Cocker Spaniels every day. He will probably bite you the next time he sees you.

MAY 29, 2018 - SALTHOUSE BRANCH REC AREA, VA

Why is driving so exhausting?

I guess that's a rhetorical question: the answer's obvious. But there's a reason most people don't spontaneously say, "Hey, let's go for a three hour drive today, won't that be fun?"

Driving slowly, with breaks of a day or two between chunks of long driving days, doesn't improve the experience. Brutal ten-hour days of driving require recovery days but so, apparently, do five-hour driving days. At least for me.

But I broke my drive from South Carolina to Pennsylvania by stopping for two nights at Salthouse Branch Recreation Area in Henry, Virginia. It was about five hours from my last stop, albeit closer to seven with stops for gas, dog walks, and lunch, so I got there on Friday with plenty of time to relax.

Along with all the rest of the people in the state who wanted a nice relaxing Memorial weekend Friday.

I believe I've complained about views that include my neighbor's trailer instead of nature? At Salthouse Branch, I could see eleven trailers from the van door. Yes, I counted.

There were also some nice looking trails, but I didn't take advantage. It was a bad combination of circumstances. First, I was tired. Second, it was hot enough that I didn't want to wear long pants and socks and hiking boots. And third, there were ticks.

So many ticks I was literally flicking them off the water hose and steps. Given the number of tick-borne diseases on the east coast, bare legs in the woods felt like a no-brainer level of stupid.

I really do hate ticks.

JUNE 30, 2018 - PROUD LAKE STATE REC AREA, MI

My blueberries were rotten this morning. I bought them yesterday, carefully scoping out the packages for one that looked good, but it was wasted effort. They were tasteless, some already soft and squishy.

I decided to take it as a sign from the universe.

The reason I was looking for signs was this:

I hated everything about this campsite. Every single thing.

To say this campsite makes me cranky would be an understatement. To say it makes Zelda uneasy would also be an understatement. I think she can hear the hum of the lines, especially at night when they sizzle because of the moisture in the air. She wanted to go out over and over again last night, but every time we went out, she only wanted to stand and stare into the darkness.

It was impressive darkness, actually — fireflies, a full moon, stars. I should give credit where it's due.

But this campground is one designed for family parties with lots of kids in tents. I'm parked on the street at the edge of my site, because it has the most extreme slope of any site I've ever had, so much so that my water jug slowly slid off the counter last night and landed on the floor. Plus, it's in full sunlight, no shade at all, and it's supposed to go up to 96 degrees today. The van is going to be an oven.

I was planning to spend the month in Michigan, but I've been struggling to find places to stay. Well, places I want to stay. There's a specific campground layout — straight lines all in rows — which after two years of camping makes my lips curl back in distaste. Give me some nice cul-de-sacs any day.

I'm also extremely wary of big campgrounds. Once you've got 150 campsites all lined up in rows, you're basically looking at traffic, people, crowds, noise, and barking dogs. For people with boats and kids, it can be a nice vacation, but I'm not on vacation.

I'm looking for quiet campsites, privacy, solitude, and beautiful views. I love the trees and the birds and the starry nights, but I don't need good places to let the kids run around with their cousins while the grown-ups sit by the fire and drink beer.

The Michigan State Parks — at least the ones with availability for people who don't plan their destinations six months in advance — all look like family vacation spots, not comfortable writing nests.

And meanwhile, I have a comfortable writing nest. My brother's garden house comes with fresh blueberries, excellent company, lots of privacy, and the chance of fun with my niece. Oh, and electricity that's given to me freely instead of costing me $28/night.

The only problem with it is that it's 10 hours away.

I think, therefore, that I should stop writing and get on the road. The universe, after all, gave me lousy blueberries this morning and the message came in loud and clear.

JULY 24, 2018 - ALLENTOWN, PENNSYLVANIA

Tomorrow marks two years since I signed the paperwork on my house and drove away. Which means today is two years since I wandered around my house, doing last-minute cleaning, having one last torchlight swim, feeling surprisingly peaceful as I said good-bye to my home and ventured out into a new life.

My brother asked me the other day if I'd take my house back if I could and I didn't even hesitate before saying, "Oh, yeah, definitely. If I could afford it. I loved my house."

But I have no regrets. It's amazing to look back on this past year, which feels like it's lasted a lifetime, and remember all the things I've done.

Campsites by the numbers:

- 8 parking lots
- 28 state parks
- 3 national parks
- 2 national forests
- 1 Department of Natural Resources
- 1 Bureau of Land Management
- 6 Army Corps of Engineers
- 4 county parks
- 1 KOA
- 3 Thousand Trails
- 1 Good Sam
- 1 independent, not affiliated with a program
- 11 driveways
- 2 streets
- 2 guest beds
- 1 air mattress in an office

If I'm counting right, 75 different places in 32 different states.

I saw Mount Rushmore and the Grand Canyon; a moose in Montana and a bear in Washington. I visited friends and family across the country. I cleaned out a refrigerator in California and organized spices in Seattle. I took a few ferries and walked on a few beaches. I got elevation sickness in Arizona and a phenomenal cold in Arkansas.

I took a lot of pictures; I wrote a lot of words.

It was a good year.

As it comes to an end, I'm not sure what the future will bring. I love experiencing a beautiful sunrise surrounded by nature, but I'm tired of needing to strategize about how to shower. I like seeing new places, but I've lost all enthusiasm for driving. But I told a friend recently that I'd failed to plan an exit strategy.

And there's still an awful lot I want to do. Vermont again, Canada, Wyoming, more time in Montana, another visit to friends in the west, another visit to friends in the northeast. I don't think I'm through adventuring.

AUGUST 4, 2018 - SOMEWHERE IN NEW YORK

I'm going to start with the good news: Zelda is going to be fine. Most likely, anyway, but let's stick with the optimistic belief for right now.

Zelda is going to be fine.

The story: I'm in a nice campground, my first New York State Park. Loads of grass, a water view, sea gulls swooping in, lots of people but big spaces so we're not all on top of one another.

I've had a good day. I sent out an email to my mailing list this morning and got some nice responses from people happy about my book release, and then I worked on my next book for a while and liked what I wrote.

In the late afternoon, it's getting toasty in the van, but there's a cool breeze outside, so I decide to take Z for a walk. We're walking along and I'm totally in my head. I don't remember what I was thinking, but I know I wasn't admiring the scenery. I was daydreaming, probably about the story I'm writing.

Suddenly a dog is jumping on Zelda.

A big dog.

And it's not playing.

It's trying to kill her.

And I hate to admit this truth, because I do think they get a bad rap, but it's a pit bull. And it is not going to let go.

I was trying to pull it off — totally willing to get bitten, not avoiding its mouth at all — its owner was trying to pull it off, a guy from a neighboring campsite was trying to pull it off, and that pit bull didn't give a damn what any of us were doing.

It had its prey in its mouth and it was keeping it.

The guy from the neighboring campsite got a piece of firewood and started hitting the pit bull and whether it was that or the owner getting a better grip on its harness, they finally got it off Zelda.

She had been bitten only once, but it was deep and bloody, all the way through her shoulder. I was shaking. So was she, probably.

Stuff happened. People talked. I wrapped myself around her and tried to breathe and tried to organize my thoughts about what needed to happen next.

The neighboring campsite guy, named John, gave me water, got a wet cloth for her, offered me a ride back to the van (eagerly accepted). He stopped on the way and reported what happened to the camp-ground host and then to the ranger. He dropped me off and I carried Zelda toward the van. She couldn't put any weight on her leg.

Some people were walking by with a small dog. I said to them, no preamble, "Where do you live? Do you live here?" The woman gave me a name, I said, "Where is that? Is it near here?"

She started describing its location, somewhere around Buffalo, I think, and I interrupted her and said, "No, too far, I need a vet here," and headed to my next door neighbor, who also had a dog. I did the same thing to her.

Within minutes, I had four or five or six people, gathered around me and Zelda. Bringing her ice and a first aid kit, finding a vet, calling an emergency vet service, handing me the phone, cleaning up the blood, bandaging her puncture, finding the one on the other side. They were so kind.

Fairly soon — also forever, but I know it was fairly soon — I was on the phone with a vet. She was about 45 minutes away, an hour given that I needed to pack up the van first, and it was after hours, so walking in the door was going to cost $175.

I packed up the van and headed off.

The vet was lovely. Truly a nice person, gentle with Zelda, and pretty gentle with me, too. She sedated Z, took x-rays to make sure her leg wasn't broken (it's not) and gave her lots of stitches. I knew antibiotics were inevitable, but when I said Z's weight was lower than usual because she hadn't been eating well, she gave her a shot instead of pills.

Z's not out of the woods. The vet was worried about nerve damage and warned me that there's going to be some deep bruising. She's probably going to be in pain for a while and we're going to have to start doing gentle exercises with her leg in four days to make sure she maintains the muscle.

But she's alive.

I'm incredibly grateful for that. We got so lucky. A fraction of an inch deeper and her lung would have been punctured. She would have died in the van on the way to the vet.

Every time I think about that, tears start rolling out of my eyes. Her story would be over today and I would be devastated.

But I'm not devastated and that's good. I'm just kind of... well, crying a lot.

Apart from that, I don't really know how I feel. People have suggested I should be angry, and maybe I should, but I don't feel it. People have told me I need to make the other dog's owner pay her vet bill, and obviously I should do that, but I don't know. I don't, can't, find the energy to make that happen. I stopped by their campsite to tell them she was going to survive and they were apologetic, but they didn't offer to pay the bill and I didn't ask. I didn't feel hostile to them, I felt sorry for them. They were in the wrong and that's their karma, not mine.

And at the end of the day, people were kind and that's what I want to remember.

But I really wish I could call my mom. Three days from now, it will be seven years since she died, but she's still the person I want when what I really need to do is cry and say how scared I was and then cry some more.

AUGUST 6, 2018 - CEDAR BEACH CAMPGROUND, CANADA

In the distance, not far away, but obscured by trees and campers, I can see a glimmer of blue. A lake. I assume it has a nice beach, because over the weekend, this campground was filled with families having fun.

I, however, haven't seen it, because Zelda makes bad choices when left alone. Bad choices!

I used to tell teenage R, when he was headed off to do things with his friends, "Make good choices," and eventually he said the same thing to me whenever I left the house. It always made me smile.

But I would scold Zelda with that phrase if I could. If I leave her on the floor, she jumps onto the seats to look out the windows, and if I leave her on a seat, she jumps to the floor so she can try a different window. She wants to be able to see me.

So no walks for me, because every jump for her causes a yelp of agony, and yet she refuses to not jump if I'm not there to stop her.

Today is seven years since my mom died. I've been thinking about her a lot, about why she's who I want when I need a shoulder to cry on. She was a brisk mother. My ex once described her as "austere," which I thought was wrong, but she could be quite dispassionate. I could cry to her and she would be warm and loving and sympathetic, but she wasn't going to take on any of my pain and she was going to stop me as soon as she decided I was wallowing.

But I didn't need to be a grown-up with her. It wasn't about love, it was about her endless ocean of calm. She was extremely good at pulling small children's loose teeth, because she didn't care how much you fussed. If you were ready to have the tooth out, she was going to yank it. If you weren't ready, she was going to shrug and leave you alone. She was a nurse, and I think she was probably excellent at her job.

There's a line in my most recent book — oh, a paragraph. I'll quote it:

Grace wished she could talk to her mom. Just for half an hour. To hear her mom's voice, to let herself be folded into her mother's hug. She could imagine the sharp, searching look her mother would give her, followed by the, "Chin up, darlin'. That's my girl," words of approval.

Pretty sure my mother never said those words to me. She wasn't a southerner and that wasn't her language. But a look, a nod, a "You'll be fine."

The confidence in me, but the hug, too.

That was my mom.

I miss her.

She would tell me to stop wallowing.

AUGUST 13, 2018 - GRAND ISLE STATE PARK, VERMONT

I made my reservations for Grand Isle several weeks ago. It's the most popular state park in Vermont, on an island in Lake Champlain, and in my imaginary visit, there was much kayaking, some swimming, some hiking — several days of actual nature adventure.

Real camping, not just living in a van.

Sadly, my imagination did not include a limping dog. But nor did it include human companions, in the form of my delightful son and my favorite cousin. So things balanced out, some bad, some good. I'm sorry to say my kayak never touched the water, and neither did Zelda or I. R walked down to the beach and went swimming but it was too long a walk for Z.

We did, however, have a campfire one night and cooked sausages over the fire, which was fun, and we went to a farmer's market where I bought maple syrup, which felt very Vermont.

And the campground was as beautiful as I'd expected it to be. Vermont is gorgeous. This was my second visit, and it's so green and hilly. I suspect I wouldn't like it nearly as much in winter, but in August, it's lovely.

After five days, R is now my longest van companion. He says he's tired of hitting his head, which I sympathize with. I don't know if he would ever want to drive around exploring the country, but I'm pretty sure if he did, he'd like a taller vehicle. The perils of being 6'4"!

But we've done well together, I think. I was worried that after a few days of tripping over each other, I'd be getting cranky about clutter and he'd be getting cranky about me being cranky, but so far, so good.

A second (and, briefly, third) person does mean a lot more dishes to wash, though, and that's meant some minor tragedies. Yesterday I broke two of my favorite bowls, because I didn't stow them properly when we were on the road, and I've been surprisingly sad about that.

When you own almost nothing, the things you own that you love become much more important, I guess. But I'm trying to remind myself that the universe has plenty of bowls, and maybe I'll find some new ones that I love just as much.

AUGUST 14, 2018 - GREEN LAKES STATE PARK, NY

R and I had no specific plans after Grand Isle, but he needs to be back in Toronto by Wednesday. Originally, I thought we'd wander through Ontario, but after much discussion, we decided to take the southern route instead.

It's longer, because we're swinging south to get below Lake Ontario and then going up the other side of the lake and around to get to Toronto, but it offered several advantages.

First, gas is enough cheaper in the US that the cost was probably close to the same.

Second, driving through the south opened up the possibility of driving by several places where I used to live. This area of upstate New

York is where I grew up and I haven't been back in decades. R's never been here.

Third, Niagara Falls! Classic Americana road trip, the kind of thing that belongs on a list with the Grand Canyon and Mount Rushmore.

We're staying now at Green Lakes State Park, which is a gorgeous park, green and lush, with pleasant treed campsites and nice showers — the single room kind, where you have a door, plus control over the water temperature.

The weather, typical of this oh-so-familiar area, is gray and gloomy, but we drove around for a while, passing by my old high school, three houses I lived in (one of which I couldn't identify — best I could do was say, " somewhere around here and now we must have passed it"), and the site of every bookstore and library I loved.

R's impression of my childhood is probably that I did nothing but go to school and read books, because those are the only things I remember. Although that said, I do vaguely recall this park as a place where we swam in the summer.

Maybe it's because I vaguely remember it that I've been feeling utterly phobic about poison ivy. I swear, every random leaf looks like a poison ivy leaf to me. Did I once get poison ivy in this park? Is that why I'm so paranoid?

That's probably not it, though. Sometimes anxiety manifests as semi-irrational fears in order to shield our minds from less-irrational fears. In this case, I think I'm struggling not to let last week's attack turn into a serious dog phobia.

It was so fast, so out-of-nowhere, so aggressive and so brutal. My head still knows that dogs are our friends, but the back of my neck seems to be experiencing some post-traumatic stress. While I try to talk myself out of it, I worry about poison ivy.

AUGUST 15, 2018 - FIFTY POINT CONSERVATION AREA, GRIMSBY, ONTARIO

I wrote the name of this campground as Conversation Area initially, which amused me. It would be so apt! Our site is a pull-through adjacent to another pull-through pointed in the opposite direction, so we're close to our neighbors but facing opposite ways. Conversation would be easy, but is not required.

The campground itself is everything I like in a campground: grass, trees, water, sunlight, space, beautiful walking, a dog beach, and birds, including the world's cutest woodpecker working on the tree by the picnic table and some unidentified species sauntering through the grass.

Even the bugs were cute. I have no idea what the one crawling on the sink this morning was, but it was green and tiny, with long legs. Maybe some kind of aphid?

Also lots of birch trees. I've decided that the wind rustling through birch tree leaves makes a unique noise. It's not the same as wind rustling through other tree leaves. The birch leaves sound like they're whispering.

And tons of cricket noise last night, or maybe frogs. But the night was loud and seventy degrees, for the perfect summer feeling.

Yesterday was Niagara Falls. It was crazily tourist-y, in the way all the main tourist attractions seem to be. Excellent people watching. That said, they were some cool waterfalls, no question about that. And it was such a hot day that standing in the spray of the mist felt great.

We also saw my earliest childhood home yesterday, only somewhat out of our way. The interesting thing about that was not so much how different the neighborhood looked from my memory — different, and so much smaller — but that I had the address wrong.

The day before, when I was failing to find my other childhood homes, I told R confidently that my early memories were the most reliable and that of all the different places I'd lived in during my child-hood, the only one I actually remembered the address of was the first.

Wrong. I had the street right, but not the number. I'm not sure that means anything, except maybe that none of my memories are reli-able. But I had a different feeling looking at that house than at the others, much warmer and cozier. I'm glad we drove by.

AUGUST 29, 2018 - CAMPING JUNEAU

When I imagined van life, one thing I didn't picture accurately — at all — was how much time I would spend looking at campground websites, campground reviews, and campground apps, trying to find places to stay.

It seemed straightforward when I started. Look for places other people liked, right?

But we all have different tastes. People who are driving 40-foot long buses have different needs than people in 20-foot camper vans. People on vacation with kids want different things than a writer with a dog. Serious athletes appreciate different qualities than casual walkers. People who are planning to spend months in one place have different goals than people who are wandering through, hoping for some time in nature.

Those last parks, the ones for people planning to spend months in one place, have the word "seasonals" in their descriptions. Over the course of the last two-plus years, I've started avoiding them.

In Florida, especially, they're the campgrounds that are long rows of trailers stacked up one next to the other, with a view of your neighbor's sewer hose. Parking spaces with lawn chairs. They curdle my soul.

On Monday, I woke up in a Walmart parking lot, did my shopping, then wasn't quite sure what to do with the rest of the day. I knew where I wanted to be on Tuesday, but I didn't have a plan for Monday night.

But it was going to be hot, so unless I wanted to drive all day or run the (obnoxiously loud) generator, I wanted electricity. I can survive a 90-degree van, Zelda cannot.

I spent a while considering my options, my energy level, and my goals, and finally decided to try an inexpensive seasonal campground. It was seasonal, but it was just for a night and it had laundry facilities. Good enough.

I drove by it, saw that it was a parking lot with lawn chairs, and decided to try my next option: a more expensive, but also seasonal campground in Quebec City.

Option #2, Camping Juneau, is adorable. Completely charming and beautiful in a campground sort of way. It isn't stylish. The buildings are a little run-down, the signs were hand-made (some of them, at least), the roads are narrow gravel and dirt, the washing machine had dead bugs on it, and my fire pit was made of crumbling concrete.

But a shack of a restaurant had a patio, maybe four tables with plastic tablecloths, overlooking the lake. There were trees between all the spaces, plants everywhere. It reminded me somehow of Maine and Greece, mixed with the resort in the Catskills from *Dirty Dancing*. Sunshine and shade and summer.

I didn't do my laundry, but I opened the awning and got out my chair, and read while sitting in the shade. I had a lovely afternoon.

I think the thing I'll look for in future campground descriptions is "tents." Juneau might have been seasonal, but it had tent spots and tent campers, and tent campers probably don't like parking lots either.

SEPTEMBER 2, 2018 - PRINCE EDWARD ISLAND

On August 31, I woke up to a beautiful sunrise in a Walmart parking lot on Prince Edward Island. The air was fresh and cool, a hint of chill, and I walked Zelda in a big patch of grass while trying to smell ocean. (I failed, but it was easy enough to smell later.)

We went to a grocery store, Atlantic Superstore, and for the first time in Canada, I found ALL the things: the dog food Zelda's most likely to eat, gluten-free oats so I can make granola, even Greek yogurt with the fat. (Fat-free Greek yogurt is the most pointlessly unpleasant food. I don't understand how people eat it. But apparently that's what they like in Canada. Not on PEI, though!)

Then I headed to Green Gables. I paid to drive through the Prince Edward Island National Park, which would have been silly except that it was a stunningly beautiful drive on a gorgeous day, well worth $4.

At Green Gables, I joined the throng of early bird tourists to admire the historic house and beautiful gardens, then escaped from them entirely for a solo walk through the Haunted Woods. They didn't feel haunted, but I'm sure my imagination could have conjured up ghosts on a dimly-lit evening. And they were probably fantastic in the days when the paths weren't lined with logs and well-trodden by thousands of feet.

The inspiration for the Haunted Woods in Anne of Green Gables.

Next I drove to the north of the island, admiring the scenery at every turn. I once told R that I was disappointed on my first trip to England, because it wasn't the brilliant green that my imagination had conjured up from years of reading. Prince Edward Island, on the other hand, is exactly that color green.

It was past lunch time and I was hungry, so I thought about

making myself a salad, like a good van lifer. Instead, I stopped, read TripAdvisor, then went to The Lobster Shack and bought myself a cold lobster and a half dozen oysters. I ate the oysters on their patio overlooking the ocean, each one with a different hot sauce, while Zelda napped at my feet. I brought the lobster with me to the campground.

At the campground, my neighbors were using my fire pit — they apologized, but I didn't mind, I didn't plan on using it myself — so I got to smell campfire smoke mixed with ocean spray.

Zelda and I went walking, taking the steps directly in front of my site down to an empty beach.

The stairs to the beach.

When she hit the sand, she ran like a puppy. She got her feet wet and yelped with surprise at how cold the water was, but we had the nicest walk we've had since she got hurt, out to the end of the curve of sand and onto red rocks, and then back again.

Back at the van, I read some *Anne of Green Gables*, eventually ate cold lobster dipped in melted butter with lime, admired the sunset, appreciated the smell of campfire smoke, and listened to the ocean.

It was a most amazing day.

Yesterday was beach, beach, more beach, interspersed with good words on the story I'm working on. There was a beautiful sunrise in a cloudy sky, and then a gray rainy morning, with the sound of rain on the van roof, the sight of dark ocean ahead of me.

Then the sky cleared and the afternoon was sunny and golden. The evening was the smell of campfires and a fantastic night sky, scattered with so many stars that if I knew anything about stars, I bet I could have found all the constellations ever named. (Except the ones that can only be seen in the Southern Hemisphere, of course.)

SEPTEMBER 6, 2018 - PRINCE EDWARD ISLAND

I leave this morning to go into "town"* to try to get my leaking toilet fixed. Tomorrow, I'm driving about an hour away from "town" in the other direction to get the oil changed and the brake fluid levels checked in the van.

The need to get this stuff done was motivating me to get moving, with some idea that the right place to take care of such things is "home."

But I was chatting with one of my neighbors yesterday and realized there should be places to take care of such things here and that once they were done, the nagging sense of obligation to get going would probably fade away.

And once that nagging sense fades away... well, maybe I'll be back at this campground. Or maybe I'll feel inspired to go explore some of Nova Scotia. I'm honestly not sure which.

But if this morning's sunrise was my last sunrise here, I'm glad I got out on the beach while it was still rising and got to feel the wind and listen to the birds and see Zelda jumping off the rocks like her leg had never been hurt at all.

*"Town" is Charlottetown. It's over an hour away, but when people say "town," that's what they mean.

Sunrise on Prince Edward Island

SEPTEMBER 8, 2018 - CABOT BEACH PROVINCIAL PARK

I've had three days of enormous efficiency and I'm exhausted. Although I think the exhaustion is because for the first time, I've got awful neighbors. Oh, wait, I just remembered some bad neighbors in New York a couple of years ago. But those neighbors were bad because

I had to eavesdrop on their complaining; these neighbors are bad because I had to eavesdrop on their late-night fun.

And by late night, I mean that sometime close to 3AM, security showed up and yelled at them, saying he could hear them all the way down by the security gate, half a mile away. Given that my van is parked about three feet away from their RV, I didn't get a lot of sleep last night.

I did entertain myself thinking of polite revenge fantasies. My favorite was to set off my smoke alarm at 7AM. I could even do it legitimately. It goes off pretty much every time I use the stove, so I wouldn't have to burn anything. I could be slow to make it stop. And then maybe I could cook something else half an hour later and do it again. I didn't do it, however, because I'm not really a revenge person.

However, if they keep me up all night again — and their music is already playing — all bets are off.

SEPTEMBER 17, 2018 - GLOOSCAP CAMPGROUND, PARRSBORO, NOVA SCOTIA

This is the first time I've sat by a beach long enough to realize that the sound of the water changes over the course of the day. Or maybe it's just this beach. The tide goes way, way out. In the middle of the day, there's half a desert between me and the water, but in the morning, it's more of a wide rocky strip.

Sometimes the water is quiet, gently brushing against the shore, so still that even listening hard I can barely hear it, and then sometimes it's lapping at the shore so loudly that I'm reminded that yes, I am sitting next to the ocean. (Sort of the ocean, anyway. I'm on the shores of the Bay of Fundy in Nova Scotia.)

The weather has been lovely. Sometimes sunny enough that it feels hot, although I doubt the temperature has broken 75, and sometimes foggy enough that it feels chilly, but mostly hovering in the mid-60s. It's the perfect level of humidity, too. It feels like there's always just a light breeze, carrying a little moisture.

Serenity's campsite at Glooscap, Nova Scotia. Just beyond her were loads of wildflowers in bright colors.

But for some reason, none of my photos are getting the colors right. An incredible number of wildflowers are blooming right now. I'm looking at an expanse of yellow-gold and green, but the photos capture the blue of the ocean behind the gold and turn the gold into a dull yellow that doesn't come anywhere close to the real thing.

And, of course, it's impossible to take a photo of the moon and the stars, but I've been watching them every night from my window as I go to sleep.

Here's a thing that made me feel stupid: over two years of living in the van, and I never realized how much the tinted windows were

The view from the van window.

distorting the brightness of the stars. I've been sleeping with the window open and they're so much more beautiful that way.

It would be nice to see the stars without the screens, too, but that's never going to happen because the one thing about Nova Scotia that is not working for me are the voracious mosquitoes. Almost every walk on the beach ends when the mosquitoes find me and I wind up needing to escape from the ones dive-bombing my face. Still, they're not constant. They're worst at dusk and dawn. In the middle of the day, I've been sitting outside happily.

Yesterday, I ate blueberry pancakes with tiny wild Canadian blueberries and Vermont maple syrup, plus Berkshire bacon from an organic farm, while sitting at a picnic table watching horseback riders on the beach. I wondered whose life was more perfect at that moment, the horseback riders splashing through the water or me, and concluded that I won because my pancakes were crazily delicious and they were probably surrounded by mosquitoes.

OCTOBER 15, 2018 - ALLENTOWN, PENNSYLVANIA

I read some sad news on Facebook, that bastion of unwelcome tidings, a few days ago. Honestly, I've started to dread looking at Facebook. It feels like a magnet for misery, at least in my feed.

My friend Suzanne's husband, Greg, passed away, quite unexpectedly. My immediate response was to pick up my phone, but my secondary response has been to spend a lot of time browsing my own history. Photographs and journals and blog posts, reminders of times past.

It made me resolve to take more pictures of human beings. I have lots of sunrises, flowers and scenery, and lots and lots of dog pictures, but not many people pictures.

I dreamed last week that Bartleby's new owner needed to give B back to me, because his circumstances had changed and he couldn't take care of B anymore. He passed him over to me and B was matted and skinny, really skinny, and I felt horrible because obviously somehow I'd given B to people who neglected him. But then I was so happy to have him back. He snuggled into my arms and I promised him an immediate bath with a long blow-dry afterwards (he loved the blow-dryer) and plenty of food.

Then I woke up.

In a way, it was a great dream, but it ruined my day.

I told Suzanne that death felt like that to me, in general. Every day you have to keep waking up into a reality that's not the one you wanted to wake up in. And there's no way to make the universe take you back to the reality you had yesterday.

8

2019 - CRISS-CROSSING THE COUNTRY

JANUARY 14, 2019 - BLUE SPRINGS STATE PARK

Last night, I left the windows open and stared up through the trees at the night sky while I was trying to sleep. It felt so nice to be back in nature: no bright street lights shining in the window, no passing cars, no sounds of people wandering by.

I've been enjoying my January. Lots of people, lots of activity, lots of dinners out and social time. This visit to Blue Springs is a continuation of the socializing: I came here to meet some fellow Travato owners and talk the camping lifestyle. We spent much of yesterday afternoon sitting around in our chairs, chatting.

But this morning, comfortably before dawn, Z and I wandered down through the campground to the boardwalk along the spring. We weren't the only people there. I bumped into a few others, including some of the Travato friends I met yesterday.

Mostly, though, it was Z and me, alone with the manatees and the birds and the squirrels, in the slightly crisp morning air.

It reminded me of why I'm living this way. Earlier this week I was browsing real estate listings in Mount Dora. Some of the older houses are authentic tiny homes. One was 760 square feet, with two bedrooms, a kitchen and a living space. The bathroom had a tub, the backyard was fenced, and the house was walking distance to the library, cute shops and restaurants, maybe even a yoga studio. What more could I want?

Answers: Manatees. Fresh air. Sunrises over water.

Adventure.

On Feb 1, I'm heading west. I'll take the southern route, through Alabama and Mississippi, then Louisiana, Texas, New Mexico and Arizona. Then I'm going to drive up the California coastline until I reach Arcata. I'll plant myself there in Suzanne's driveway for a while. Long enough to help her clean out the storage shed and Greg's office, and keep her company through the darkest months of the year.

JANUARY 28, 2019 - SOMEWHERE IN FLORIDA

Yesterday was a torrential rain day. I never got out of my pajamas and I spent far too much time playing Candy Crush.

At about 6 PM, I thought, "I have wasted my day! I should..." and then I stopped myself.

A decade ago, I could easily have taken a rainy Sunday as a chance to do nothing much. To watch some television, putter around the house, play some video games, maybe read a book. At 6 PM, I might have felt guilty enough about my laziness to throw a load of laundry in the washer, but I might not have, too.

Somehow life in a van and, I suppose, self-employment makes me feel like I have to do things every day. All the things. I have to run errands and write words and go for good walks and check social media and answer email and read books and work on becoming a better meditator/writer/photographer/cover designer.

But yesterday was just a lazy day. It was chilly and wet and the van was cozy and it was nice to be snuggled under the covers with Zelda on my feet. I have no regrets. As I look at my week ahead — a busy week, which I expect to end in some other state, maybe Texas? — I'm glad I appreciated my rainy day as an opportunity to do nothing.

FEBRUARY 4, 2019 - BEAVER DAM CAMPGROUND, KISATCHIE NATIONAL FOREST

I had grand plans: I was going to get ALL the things done. Writing and email and updating files, cleaning the van, cooking for the whole week ahead.

Funny thing, spending two solid days driving does not motivate one to get ALL the things done. It motivates one to pick things up and then set them down again, in a helplessly fluttery, "can't keep track of what I was doing for more than ten seconds" mode.

I was helped in my useless state by having it be a gray day in a mostly deserted national forest. All around me were barren trees and dead leaves. Beautiful nature, but beautiful in a bleak way.

Beautiful in a "nice day for warm beverages and soup" way.

But let me backtrack. I left Florida on Friday, not crazily early but reasonably early. I intended a long driving day, but I'd had a mostly sleepless night of anticipation.

I have no idea why I was so wound up about leaving, but I was. When I was trying to fall asleep, it was as if I needed to wake up early to catch the last helicopter out of the city before the invading army arrived.

Win one for the anxious brain.

But the mindful brain got the last laugh: instead of stressing the next day, I forced myself to relax. I took my time, ate a good lunch, let Zelda enjoy the rest stops to her heart's content.

Well, almost. I'm pretty sure Zelda would spend forever in a rest stop if I let her. It's got to be like an art museum for dogs, or maybe a theme park. So many interesting smells! So much to sniff! Eventually I made her get back in the van, but first I let her check out far more of the trees than I usually do.

Eventually, well after dark, I pulled into a Cracker Barrel parking lot outside of Mobile, Alabama. There was only one other camper there: an older one, run-down, with a For Sale sign in the window that read "Runs Good, $5000."

I considered whether I wanted to stay. Deciding whether a parking lot is going to be an okay place to spend the night sometimes feels like a balancing act. Quiet is good; isolated is not. Well-lit is appealing for safety, terrible for sleeping. Litter, broken glass, and graffiti are all red flags.

I'd already walked Z at a rest stop, which is typically what I do when I'm going to overnight in a parking lot. Once at the parking lot, if it passes my Spidey-sense inspection, I pull down the blinds and close the cab curtain, do whatever I need to do, and go to bed without leaving the van. Before I fall asleep, I make sure everything is put away, cabinets and fridge latches closed, so that if I do need to leave in the middle of the night, I'm ready to go.

This parking lot felt fine. Maybe a little isolated, but peaceful and clean. So I went to bed.

The next morning, bright and early, not quite 7AM, I walked Zelda around the parking lot. I checked out the Cracker Barrel hours, thinking I might grab breakfast there. But on my way back to the van, an older man in a cowboy hat approached me.

Being approached by a strange guy in an isolated parking lot always produces an adrenaline surge.

But he apologized immediately. "I'm sorry to bother you, ma'am, but my battery's dead. Do you think I could get a jump?"

I hesitated, wondering how deeply my jumper cables were buried.

"I'm harmless, I promise," he added.

I chuckled and said, "I am, too." Then I said I was wondering about cables and he assured me that he had his own.

It took us a while to figure out what we were doing. We were on the verge of giving up when I pulled up a youtube video on my phone and we learned that we were doing it right, we just needed patience. I ate breakfast sitting in *Serenity*'s driver's seat with the engine on, and George's camper finally rumbled back to life.

I think George and I were almost equally satisfied when his camper was finally running: him, because hey, he was no longer stuck in a parking lot, and me because it felt great to be able to help him.

Well, and also because he wasn't a serial killer, lying about his dead battery in order to hit me over the head and murder me horribly.

The anxious brain was wrong! Win another one for the mindful brain.

So my Saturday started off well and it continued well. The driving was... driving. Not much to say about it. Sometimes I admired the scenery; sometimes I developed complicated speeches to convince people of the rightness of my political philosophies; sometimes I contemplated systems to quickly determine whether a number is prime or not; sometimes I worked on stories (although never the one I meant to be working on); sometimes I got in the zone and just drove.

Around 3 or so, I started considering whether I should pay for a campground for the night or whether I should just push on for another few hours, find a parking lot, and look for a campground for the next day. Since I'm at a campground, it's probably obvious that I went for the former.

Knowing I'm going to be driving 3100 miles in the next two weeks makes me reluctant to take lengthy detours, though. I'd been looking at an Army Corps of Engineers campground, but when it came down to it, I didn't want to drive as far away from the highway as it would have required. Round trip, it would have added 52 miles to my journey. Not a huge number, but approximately 1.67% of the total.

(Along with the political arguments, I spent an inordinate amount of time on my drive calculating gas costs, mileage, and whether cruise control was economically prohibitive. Answer: Yes, although not if my entire drive could take place in Mississippi and Alabama where gas prices are delightfully low.)

Anyway, all that to explain how I ended up in this national forest. At night, there were no lights at all. The darkness is impressively dark. I could wish for clearer skies, because the stars might be amazing, but the darkness is kind of amazing too. Most campgrounds are not really dark, because of all the ambient people light — lights on campers, lights on bathrooms, sometimes even streetlights in the campground. Not this one. Across the water, one lone light is shining, but it doesn't even make a dent in the blackness. It makes me look forward to getting out west and camping in the desert.

FEBRUARY 8, 2019 - PALO DURO CANYON, TEXAS

I'm sitting at the bottom of a canyon in Texas and it is cold. For the first time, the van couldn't keep up with the chill during the night.

That was mostly my fault. I know how to conserve heat in the van: curtain off the cab, close the bathroom doors, and put the shades down and the window covers up. Not complicated.

I didn't do it, though, because hello, canyon. Beautiful isolated rocky cliffs, incredible dark starry night, and the only light that which came from all the myriad ridiculous little lights that shine in the van all night long.

At night, the stars were incredible.

FEBRUARY 11, 2019 - NEEDLES, CALIFORNIA

The van started making a weird noise while I was driving yesterday, so I did what all grown-ups do when their vehicles start making weird noises: I called my dad.

He said, "That sounds like a tire problem, probably a loose lug nut. Get off the highway."

At various points in the last few days, I have been very much in the middle of big deserts and extended mountain ranges: Texas, New Mexico, Arizona, and finally into California, and so my protest was automatic. "But I'm in the middle of nowhere."

Even as we spoke, though, I saw the signs for an exit up ahead. Said exit wasn't just an exit, it had an AutoZone immediately off the ramp. Yay! A place to buy a tool to tighten the loose lug nut. I drove into the parking lot, got out and looked at my wheel.

Hmm. "Loose" applied but only to the lug nuts that were left. Two of them were missing.

Inside the store, I chatted with the nice guy, who came out and took a look at the van and said, "You've been driving on that? Don't do that anymore."

He went back inside, talked to his manager, and sent me across the street to the Shell station. The nice guy at the Shell station said, "Whoa. That's not good. You might have a real problem." He jacked the van up, took the tire off, looked at the remaining lug nuts and said, "You were about five miles from disaster. And I mean a real disaster."

The nice thing about being five miles from disaster is that the actual disaster didn't happen. As a result, though, I'm now hanging out in Needles, waiting to find out how much new wheel studs are going to cost me and when they'll get here.

I got new tires right before I left Florida. Apparently, you should check the tightness of the lug nuts after driving 1000 miles, which I didn't know. Lesson learned. I'm glad it was not a much, much more painful lesson, as it truly might have been.

Also though, I'm awed by my luck. On a 3000 mile drive, the five miles before my disaster included a highway exit, an AutoZone, and a Shell station with a mechanic who could look at my van.

Doesn't that seem a lot like a miracle?

FEBRUARY 15, 2019 - HALF MOON BAY, CALIFORNIA

We have an immense mud puddle right outside the van door. There's no way for Zelda to avoid it when leaving the van. She doesn't mind — she's perfectly happy to wade in the water. But muddy dog + small van = sad dog mom.

Also, I am so tired that it took me three tries to spell the word "puddle." I nearly went into that space where it stopped feeling like a real word. Puddle? Pubble? Pebble? What's that thing called again?

I'm currently at Half Moon Bay State Beach, which is a pleasant— also, currently, extremely muddy — campground just south of San Francisco. Tomorrow, I'm going to drive into San Francisco. When I started planning this journey, I wanted to take a couple days and play in the city. But the closer I got, the more I stumbled over the reality of traveling with a large van and a small dog.

Like every city, San Francisco has terrible parking. The sensible thing to do would be to leave the van outside the city and take public transit. Except what would I do with Zelda? I'm can't leave her alone in the van for that long. So I'm going to give San Francisco a try, but I'm not going to stress myself out.

Then one more weekend on the road, but by Monday, I'll be settling down in Arcata, ready to get back to writing. I tried today, even managed to pull off a few words, but I currently can't spell puddle, so it's not exactly going well.

FEBRUARY 19, 2019 - LIBERTY GLEN, CALIFORNIA

I left Half Moon Bay on Friday morning and prayed on the drive into the city to find a parking place.

Out loud.

I apologized to the universe for asking for favors — I have a strict policy of only praying in gratitude and appreciation, and to ask for blessings for other people — but I was envisioning driving around and around in *Serenity*, finding only parking spots that would require parallel parking in tiny spaces.

Instead, there was an open parking space — not parallel! — a block away from the restaurant where I was meeting a friend.

Yes, it felt like another miracle. A really nice, very minor miracle. I envisioned my guardian angel patting themself on the back in that pleasure you feel when you find someone the perfect gift.

After lunch, S and I went to Golden Gate Park and took Zelda for a good walk, and then I dropped S off sort of close to the de Young Museum and headed north across the Golden Gate Bridge. I debated going to the Museum myself, but I wanted to get to my campground before dark.

Zelda was eager to explore the hills of Sonoma.

Good call. The campground was remarkably isolated, considering it was in Sonoma. No cell service, no electricity, and a steep and winding road in lousy condition to narrow, hilly campsites. Also mostly deserted. On Friday afternoon, I wasn't even sure I wanted to stay.

Zelda had no such doubts. She was bouncy and excited, loving the weather, cold and sunny, and the smells. So we stayed through Sunday morning, with a mostly quiet Saturday. On Sunday, I finished my long drive.

My journey lasted seventeen days, and over 3000 miles. Some parking lots, some driveways, some campgrounds. I've driven across the country four times now, with timetables ranging from four days (not solo) to about eight weeks. Seventeen days was probably too fast — I'm ready to not drive for a while and I was pretty tired by the end — but I think I managed a good balance of driving days and restful days.

FEBRUARY 25, 2019 - ARCATA, CALIFORNIA

I was warned that Arcata was a chilly, gray, foggy sorta place. I'm not sure any level of warning would have prepared me, though.

In defense of my weather shock, my weather app keeps sending me warnings. Severe Weather Advisory! Area Flood Watch! Flooding rain will cause hazardous travel. Hard Freeze Warning in effect. Etcetera. Nine warnings over the past few days, which I think means this weather is not normal.

Yesterday, I ventured out of the van exactly twice, both times to walk Zelda, both times in the pouring rain, because it wasn't possible to wait for the rain to stop. Or rather I did wait for the rain to stop and finally gave up.

Fortunately, I like hanging out in my tiny home listening to the rain. Poor Z does not like the way I've been walking her, though, because I've been carrying her from the van to the street and back again. She thinks it's undignified and wiggles to get down, but I think muddy dog footprints all over my bed can only happen once in a while, not twice a day, every day.

Last night, I was cozy in the van, snuggled up under my covers, when Suzanne texted me, "Warm muffins and ice cream...?"

That would be a yes.

I pulled on a hoodie, slipped on my shoes and hurried into the house where I ate a gluten-free huckleberry muffin fresh out of the oven with some vanilla bean ice cream. Yum.

Over our warm muffins and ice cream, Suzanne and I talked about plans. I'm ostensibly here to help with the post-bereavement cleaning out and organizing. It's a big job.

But I think the more important reason I'm here, at least for this moment, is to be an escape companion. Suzanne wants distractions. She wants to go places. She's working full-time, so we're mostly talking about quick adventures up in Oregon — Ashland, Medford, Gold Beach. I'm hoping the weather becomes more reasonable, because traveling with three dogs is sufficiently challenging without them being three wet, muddy dogs.

MARCH 14, 2019 - ARCATA, CALIFORNIA

I think I've now hit the longest I've stayed in one place in the van. Not the longest I've stayed in a given place, which is probably my brother's house or Christina's driveway, both with multiple repeat visits. And even Oscar Scherer State Park might have more total days.

But my longest time of staying still without some campground escape or move to another location.

I'm loving it, actually. I've thought before that when not moving, the disadvantages of living in a van so outweigh the advantages that it's simply not worth it. Without the travel, van life is life in a metal box.

But in Arcata, it's life in a metal box with yoga down the street, a farmer's market on Saturdays, a nearby beach, meditation classes, gardening and chickens, a writer's group, used bookstores, trips to Costco, a grocery store in easy walking distance with good gluten-free bread, and this week some sunshine, too.

No Oregon adventures yet, but as I said to Suzanne, why drive two hours to go to a campground by the beach, when we could drive ten minutes to the beach, then come home and cook something scrumptious in the kitchen?

Plus, we can then use the money we would have spent on a campground to rent kayaks or take kayaking lessons. Or maybe sailing lessons. Or maybe both. A place 15 minutes away rents equipment so instead of driving to Oregon this weekend, we're going to go investigate.

Yesterday was the first test of all three dogs in the van. We loaded them up and took them north on 101 to a rest stop. An exciting adventure! (Not really.)

But the rest stop had an RV dump station, so I dumped the tanks while Suzanne and the dogs wandered in the redwoods.

The dogs did okay. Zelda shared the dog bed between the seats with Riley without complaint, and Buddy took the bed in the back almost the moment he entered the van. Riley was the only one who seemed anxious, but even he relaxed after a while.

On the way back to Arcata, we stopped in Trinidad. We got coffee at a cafe and drank it on their patio, dogs in attendance, while an early morning (-ish, it was around 10) musician set up and started to play. The fog began to burn off and the sun came out. It felt like spring and smelled like ocean and redwood forest and plants.

When I woke up this morning, I asked Alexa for a weather report. She used the phrase, "lots of sun." I like that phrase so much! In Florida, it's easy to take the sun for granted. Arcata is teaching me appreciation.

APRIL 1, 2019 - ARCATA, CALIFORNIA

I told Suzanne recently that thinking of her as my former co-worker felt wrong, like it was a story missing many pieces. Once upon a time, we had cubicles down the row from one another, but that doesn't really explain how we got here.

Even back then, we were travel buddies. When our company sent us to Hawaii, we visited the rain forest and went snorkeling at a black sand beach. When our company sent us to Lake Tahoe, we went horseback riding.

When our boss needed to find out some information that she couldn't get any other way (pre-internet), we rented a car and drove to Death Valley. We've been to Belize, Key West, Disneyworld, and the

British Virgin Islands together. Sailing and snorkeling and hiking and wandering.

When I knew I was going to be staying in Arcata for a while, I went looking for an adventure for us. I sent her a link to a full day of river kayaking, then said, "Maybe that's too much?"

I think Suzanne is constitutionally incapable of saying no to an adventure. She said yes, we registered, and on Wednesday, we went to the first part of the class: learning how to get out of a kayak after you've turned it over.

The class was held in the Arcata swimming pool and was a nice intro to the idea that maybe this was going to be a scarier adventure than I'd envisioned.

I like kayaking, but I'm a cautious kayaker. (Yes, I'm cautious about everything.) Kayaking on the St. Johns, the slowest river in the US, is about my speed.

This was not that kind of kayaking. This was the kind of kayaking where you wear a wet suit and a helmet and a PFD (personal flotation device) and the kayak has a sleeve over the seat opening to prevent your boat from filling with water as you splash your way down a fast-flowing river.

Kayaking

This was the kind of kayaking where you find your way into a safe eddy and pull over to consider the risks of the next stretch of water.

This was the kind of kayaking where the instructors shout "Paddle harder, paddle harder! Paddle, paddle!!" to keep you from running smack into hazards in the water.

It was extremely fun.

Also, as Suzanne and I agreed at dinner, way outside our comfort zones. Fun, yes, but also a certain amount of scary and a fair amount of discomfort and a lot of uncertainty.

I mention that because I don't want to exclude the hard stuff or make it seem easier than it was. Worth doing, hoping to do again, but the moment halfway through when I thought, "I am so ready to be done with this," was just as real as the moment when I got through some rough water and thought exultantly, "YES! Made it!"

APRIL 8, 2019 - ARCATA, CALIFORNIA

I woke up this morning feeling disinclined to engage with the day.

The preceding sentence, both in structure and content, is what happens when you're reading too much marketing advice. Bah.

I keep promising myself that I'm going to work on that piece of the self-publishing puzzle — really, truly, any day now — but it makes me want to go back to bed. The crawl under the covers and not re-emerge until summer going back to bed, not the snooze for an extra ten minutes going back to bed.

Despite my disinclination to engage with the day, a cute little furry face bouncing around at the end of the bed was persistent enough that I dragged myself up and took her for a walk in the rain.

I thought it was just drizzle when we left the van, but it quickly became clear that it was rain-rain. The kind that's going to sop through your shoes and soak your socks; force you to keep your head down or get water in your eyes; turn your blue jeans into deadweights with minutes.

Bizarrely enough, it was satisfying. It fit my mood so perfectly. I was grouchy to begin with and there I was, getting soaked and uncomfortable and cold — it was like the universe agreeing with me, it was a day to stay in bed.

The nicest thing about today's rain is that it was supposed to be yesterday's rain. The weather forecast for yesterday was bleak, and it was both my birthday and Suzanne's day off, which meant bleak was annoying.

As it turned out, the weather didn't reach us as scheduled, so we had an early morning opportunity to fulfill my birthday wish and take Zelda to the beach. The only thing better than taking a puppy to the beach is taking an old dog to the beach and watching her run around like a puppy.

APRIL 22, 2019 - ARCATA, CALIFORNIA

Yesterday morning, I had just settled into a long-distance writing sprint with my friend Lynda — timer set and everything — when Suzanne appeared outside my door and said, "Beach?"

I don't think Suzanne should be going to the beach, because she has pneumonia and is the sickest I've ever seen her, but she swore beach air would be good for her. I remain unconvinced — she's definitely no healthier from the experience — but it was a beautiful day to be at the beach.

And so fun. Zelda tolerates other dogs, but she's usually not particularly interested in them. She and Riley, however, seem to be becoming actual dog friends.

It's odd, because he's peed on her head multiple times — she finds a good scent, he comes over to check it out, and she's still sniffing when he lifts his leg and adds his scent to the original. I object loudly every time this happens, but Z doesn't seem to care until I'm scrubbing her head when we get back to the house, and then she's displeased.

Personally, I would find being peed on to preclude friendship, but apparently dogs are more flexible. Anyway, Suzanne and I found some nice rocks to sit on and Riley and Zelda wandered off exploring together, while Buddy bounced around introducing himself to the other dogs on the beach.

It was an excellent beach visit. I should feel guilty about not writing, but I don't.

APRIL 29, 2019 - PANTHER FLAT, CALIFORNIA

I started my Saturday feeling stressed: so many things to do, so much to organize, gotta get ready to go, go, go...

Then I kicked myself and said, "Nope. Not doing this that way."

S and I were heading off on an Idaho adventure that night, but this vacation is not a scheduled, structured, must-do plan. There is no agenda, no planes to miss or clock to punch. This vacation is a wander-around, have-fun, enjoy-our-time together ramble.

So instead of spending my Saturday feeling stressed, I wrote some words, enjoyed the sunshine, and along the way, baked granola, packed the van, and got ready to go.

A much nicer day, and probably no different in accomplishment but totally different in experience.

When S got home from work at 4:30, I was ready to go and by a little after 5, we were on the road. A winding drive along the coast and through the redwoods as the sun went down led to Panther Flat Campground, in the Smith River National Recreation Area. $15 for a nice-sized site, reasonable bathrooms, easily accessible water, and plenty of trash and recycling bins.

I made blueberry pancakes for dinner, and it was so nice that Suzanne didn't set up her tent, just set out her camping pad and sleeping bag and slept under the trees. As I went to sleep in the van, I thought, "I should really sleep outside sometime."

At about 2AM, I was awake, so I opened the windows and admired the distant stars — bright but hidden behind the redwoods — until I got chilled and thought how nice it was to have a heated, comfy van to stay in. I'm probably not going to start sleeping outside any time soon.

MAY 6, 2019 - CELEBRATION PARK, IDAHO

In a world with unlimited time, I think Suzanne and I both would have liked to visit Craters of the Moon National Monument, one of Idaho's highlights. For that matter, I would also have liked to go opal mining in Spencer and visit the incredibly cute Little Library in Coeur d'Alene.

So much to do, so many, many places to go.

By Thursday morning, however, I was tired of driving and worried about the long drive back to Arcata. Unlimited time was a luxury we didn't have. Instead of pushing on and adding more miles to the trip, we decided to take it easy and enjoy where we were by exploring the Snake River Birds of Prey conservation area.

The area is huge and we touched only the tip of the iceberg by driving a couple hours to Celebration Park, a county park that felt like a good starting place to figure out where to go and what to look at in the conservation area.

In fact, it was both a good starting place and a good ending place, because the park allowed camping in their parking lot, with a river view and even better, a view of a nest of golden eagles. There were also petroglyphs, a historic bridge, and a boat ramp where the dogs could splash into the water.

And did I mention that I was tired of driving? After visiting the visitor center at the park, we drove gingerly down an incredibly bumpy dirt road to start our exploring, then said, "You know, that was a really nice parking lot."

Instead of continuing on, we went back to the parking lot and enjoyed a quiet afternoon.

MAY 8, 2019 - SUCCOR CREEK, OREGON

As we drove away from Celebration Park, Suzanne said to me, "I don't know about you, but that was the best parking lot I ever camped in."

I laughed, as expected, because it was also the first parking lot Suzanne had ever camped in.

But then I considered the idea, thinking about all the parking lots I've stayed in, from the first terrifying night in a West Virginia arts center, to Walmarts and Flying Js, a rest stop in Oregon, Cabela in Montana, a Cracker Barrel in Alabama, even the miserable night sitting outside the emergency vet longing for good news about Bartleby.

And I had to agree, Celebration Park was the nicest parking lot I've camped in.

But one night in a parking lot was plenty and then it was time to head back into Oregon. Suzanne was excited to go thunder egg hunting.

Thunder eggs, (basically rounded rocks with crystals inside), are the state rock of Oregon. She picked Succor Creek State Natural Area Campground as the place to go to find some. Sounded fine to me, but I should have made her drive.

Or maybe not. It might have made me incredibly nervous to have my home in someone else's hands as we made our way down bumpy dirt roads for what felt like hours. Even more incredibly nervous than I was with my home in my own hands.

At one point, we hit a deep spot in the road, filled with water, ridged on either side, with deep tracks from other vehicles, and if it hadn't meant I'd have to drive ten miles back over the same roads, I might have just said no.

Instead, we kept going.

It was totally worth it.

At the end of 15 miles of dirt road (predicted by Siri to take an hour of driving time), we reached an almost empty campground. We found a great spot, backing on a beautiful creek, and spent the afternoon there, enjoying the sunshine as the campground slowly filled up with people.

The slowly filling up with people part was surprising — this campground was remote — but it was a beautiful Friday in spring, so it probably shouldn't have been. I was glad we'd gotten there early, though, because we had a nice spot with enough room for Suzanne to comfortably set up her tent and we also had the fun of having the area to ourselves for a while.

It was a long drive, but the destination was worth it. Look close and you can see Serenity's campsite.

We walked the dogs and then Suzanne climbed the hills and hunted for rocks. I started up the hill, but as I clambered over the rocks, I couldn't help thinking that the rocks were a perfect place for rattlesnakes.

And that if I was a rattlesnake on a sunny warm day in spring, with temperatures reaching the 80s, I would probably be out sunning myself on the rocks.

And that as a human being, I could keep a careful eye out for snakes, but that the darling dog trailing along with me would probably not understand that a snake was dangerous.

And that if I was bitten by a rattlesnake, approximately ninety minutes away from any medical care, I'd have a chance of surviving, but that a 16-

pound dog would probably not last long enough to get to the emergency vet. As a result, instead of searching the hills for interesting rocks, Zelda and I retreated to the comfort of the grassy creekside and I read a book.

Did I let anxiety win? Maybe. But it was a lovely day and I thoroughly enjoyed my book, so maybe I kept my dog safe and happy and didn't miss anything much. It wasn't like I'd be willing to load up *Serenity* with rocks, even if I found the coolest rocks ever.

That night, we finally did something I'd been yearning to do ever since I got the idea: we built a fire and barbecued Easter peeps. They were as delicious as I'd imagined they would be — crispy carmelized sugar on the outside, melty marshmallow on the inside.

Zelda was content to sit in the shade, and I was happy to read my book in the sunshine.

MAY 10, 2019 - SOMEWHERE IN OREGON

Succor Creek was a beautiful place to wake up. The scenery on all sides was incredible.

Even the herds of small children roaming the hills couldn't make the campground feel crowded. But we had miles to go and prepaid reservations at our next campground, so we packed up and headed out.

Ironically — or in just a not-very-funny coincidence — after all my worries about driving on the dirt roads, I managed to crunch poor *Serenity* after we got back on the road.

At a gas station, sadly.

Plus, I managed to break the kind of streak everyone should wish for: thirty-five years of never having to call an insurance company because of something I'd done. Dang.

Poor *Serenity*.

But it was what it was. The van was still drivable and no one was hurt so after spending some time chatting with my truly delightful Progressive customer service person (sympathetic! helpful! organized!), we got back on the road.

Fortunately, our destination was exactly the kind of place you want to be when you're feeling stressed and frustrated with yourself: Crystal Crane Hot Springs Campground.

The campground itself was not beautiful. Dry grass, rocky gravel sites, no trees or separation between sites, and port-a-potty type toilets right across from our own site.

But the hot spring was fantastic. It was essentially a pond in the middle of the desert, and the water was amazing. Suzanne and I swam once in the afternoon, then as soon as it started to get dark we went back again. Drifting in the hot water in the cool night air while the stars came out was spectacular. Bats swooped overhead, which doesn't sound like it should be cool, but really was, and planes left contrails in the sky until it got so dark that you couldn't see them.

It was a moment where I was intensely glad to be where I was, to be alive, to be experiencing life.

MAY 13, 2019 - ARCATA, CALIFORNIA

I thought it was going to be really hard to leave Arcata this week. I'm so going to miss Suzanne and the dogs, the yoga studio down the street, the incredible gluten-free bread, the nearby beach, the friendly neighbors, even Gina, the cat that yells at me all the time. (She yells at everyone all the time, I don't think it's personal.)

The weather, however, is being obliging about encouraging me to go. It's cold and gray, in the 40s and 50s, with rain predicted all week. I'll be sorry to say good-bye, but I can't say I'm going to mind finding some sunshine.

I do have mixed feelings, though. I'm looking forward to doing all sorts of things in the next couple of months: visiting friends and family, including a mini-reunion with some college friends; meeting my brother's new puppy; eating blueberries straight from the bushes...

But I'm completely unenthusiastic about the driving part.

I'm obviously not done traveling, because I live in a van and it's not an option to not travel, but the process of getting to the places I want to go doesn't fill me with joy. I'm going to have to work on that somehow.

But one day at a time, right? Today's job is to write some words, work on getting a part ordered to fix the damage to the van, maybe schedule an oil change for later in the week. And spend as much time as possible admiring Suzanne's garden, which is fantastically beautiful right now. More so on a sunny day, but the rhododendron outside the van's window is stunning even in the gray.

Yesterday, I took Zelda and Riley for a walk down to the railroad tracks. While we were there, we met a chocolate Lab from the nearby wood-working shop. Zelda was busy sniffing some interesting plant and when this Lab came toward her, she ignored it. The Lab behaved like a typical dog, sniffing her thoroughly, head-to-butt, but Zelda offered no return sniffs, no acknowledgment.

When she finally turned away from the plant she was sniffing, she actually walked underneath the Lab, still not showing any sign of noticing it was there. I wanted to believe it was a ghost dog, but I think it's just more evidence of my girl's dementia.

I do wish I could see inside her mind. She has good days and bad days, these days, and on the good days, she's fine: bouncy and happy and playful and inquisitive, the way she's always been.

On the bad days, she's foggy. On a foggy day, she is utterly untrustworthy. She can and will wander into the street; she will get lost in the backyard; she gets very distressed if she can't find me (and sometimes doesn't realize when I'm right next to her); she doesn't show any sign that she can hear me call; and she doesn't eat.

She sleeps more than she used to, too, which is saying something, given how much dogs sleep. On the spectrum of terms for age, I feel like she's moved past "senior" and is slowly sliding from "old" to "elderly." She's only 14, and Jack Russell terriers can live to be much older than that, but... well, the good days still outnumber the bad.

Meanwhile, though, she is sleeping on my feet and we're going to the beach this afternoon and I am so grateful that she's still with me. It's been a year since she was diagnosed with canine dementia and our year has included far more happiness and far more fun than I could possibly have predicted then.

I have to remember that fearing the future just gets in the way of appreciating the day I'm in.

MAY 31, 2019 - SOMEWHERE IN MONTANA

On Wednesday, I started driving again. Along the way, I found my joy.

To be honest, I hadn't realized I'd lost it until it was back. It's not that I've been down. I'm quite upbeat most of the time.

In fact, the terms "ray of sunshine" and "living your best life" have both been used to describe me recently. Really!

But content, happy, enjoying myself, serene — all of those are quite different from the hum of joy that hit me on Wednesday.

I'm attributing it to Montana, because Montana is beyond awesome. I had forgotten that. I mean, I remembered that when I went through Montana before, I liked it a lot, enough that I hoped to come back and spend more time, but by the time I was planning this drive-through, I was thinking of it as, well, a place to drive through. An impediment on my road to friends in the east and time to write a book.

Instead, it's ridiculously gorgeous. I was unenthusiastic about driving, but it's so beautiful I couldn't help enjoying myself. Green hills and mountains and pine trees, rugged cliffs and then sprawling plains, horses and cows and cute little Western towns.

I wasn't sure where I was going for the first couple hours, but when I hit St. Regis, I didn't make the turn toward Glacier. I do want to go there someday, but in that moment, it felt like it was a check-mark on a list of places instead of fun. And I was in the mood for fun.

So instead, I went back to the sapphire mine near Phillipsburg. I bought myself a bucket of gravel and spent a pleasant hour playing in the muddy water, and then retreated to their campground in the hills, where I did nothing. Except feel happy and pleased with the world and full of joy, as I made my dinner and washed my dishes, and hung out with my dog.

It's dry camping, and by dry, I do mean dry. Their website said they had water available by the parking lot, which was technically true, but it wasn't close enough to the parking lot that I could use it to fill *Serenity*'s tank. If I'd been desperate, I could have filled a jug or two, but the woman at the mine said she wouldn't drink it, so I didn't bother.

By now, I travel with four gallon jugs of water lining the floor between the beds. Three years ago, that would have seemed like a lot of water, but not anymore. Between the generator, the van's engine, and my solar panel, I never worry about electricity, and I actually appreciate my days without internet (as long as they don't happen too often), but it's impossible to go a day without water. So I wasn't desperate, but I was careful, washing my dishes with my spray bottles and not washing myself at all.

As a result, my plan for Thursday evolved. Quite nicely, too.

JUNE 3, 2019 - BOZEMAN HOT SPRINGS RESORT

On Thursday, I headed off, so optimistic about all the things that I was going to fit into my day. Finding water was number one, but I also needed groceries and windshield wiper fluid. Of course, I'd have to buy gas somewhere — it's a daily occurrence when driving this much — and after a few nights without plugging into electricity, it would be useful to find a spot where I wouldn't feel bad about running the (obnoxiously loud) generator for an hour or so to recharge my computer.

Long story short, by 5 PM, I was tired, frustrated, sick of driving, and had at least another hour of driving to get to where I'd been hoping to spend the night.

And I still needed water.

But then there, practically calling my name, was the Bozeman Hot Springs Resort.

It had only one problem: it was the most expensive campground I'd ever considered staying at.

On the other hand, it also had one incredible virtue: with an overnight stay, you got a pass to the hot springs. These springs were swimming-pool/hot-tub style, and easy walking distance from the campground. There were 9 different pools, or maybe 10. (I feel like I remember 6 inside, and I know there were 4 outside.) It also had live music, with a singer-guitarist on a stage in front of one of the outside pools. Fancy!

And for tired, frustrated, camping-dirty me, totally worth the $64 I spent on my campsite. I took a shower, soaked in all of the hottest pools, then took another shower. Hot water, such a luxury!

JUNE 5, 2019 - YELLOWSTONE NATIONAL PARK

Want to know how to find a grizzly bear in Yellowstone National Park? Just look for the traffic jam.

Sadly, that's not a joke. I didn't take any pictures of the grizzly bear I saw, because I would have had to park along the road with dozens of other cars and my picture would have been a brown shape lumbering away in the distance. Still, it was cool to see.

I also didn't take any pictures of any of the elk I saw, not even the baby, or the mama bison with her baby for roughly the same reason. The baby bison was so cute, though. Baby bison are adorable.

Yellowstone has plenty of places to pull off the road and take photos, but on a Saturday in June, they were usually crowded. I admired the animals on my slow drive-bys, but I didn't stop.

I took this picture of a bison because it was right next to the campground. No parking required.

It was still incredibly beautiful. And immense! I knew in my head how big Yellowstone is (bigger than the smallest two states), but driving through it makes that a lot more obvious. It felt like I was driving through a state, one with spectacular scenery, snow-capped mountains, gorgeous blue lakes, and plenty of trees. Also crowds of people.

As it turned out, the crowds were not a disadvantage for me. On Saturday, I managed to snag a camping spot at Norris Campground. The spot was small and slightly sloped, and the campground was full, but it was still Yellowstone.

My Sunday plan was to leave early and head to Old Faithful,

hoping to beat the crowds there. Even if all had gone as planned, I suspect I wouldn't have beaten the crowds.

And all did not go as planned. As I drove away from my campsite, the van started making a funny noise.

My first thought was that I'd left something loose in the back. I paused and did a quick check. What could be rattling around? But the silverware drawer (always a likely suspect) was closed, and there was nothing visibly loose. So I drove a little farther.

Nope, definitely a weird noise. Paused the van again and checked the fan. Could something have gotten stuck in it? I turned the fan off, in case it was a problem with the cover rattling.

I started driving again and it was clear that turning the fan off had done nothing. So I paused again, in the middle of the road, and got out to walk around the van.

The problem was obvious as soon as I crouched down and looked underneath. A metal bracket was dragging on the ground. I think — and I'm mostly guessing — I think it's a bracket for the generator. Whatever it is, it's not the kind of thing that you want scraping along the ground, instead of doing its job.

I thought bad words. I thought about wire and duct tape and zip ties and bungee cords. I thought about finding RV service places in the middle of an enormous park, at least fifty miles away from anything, and how much it was likely to cost to have someone come fix it, but how bad it could be if that piece stopped doing its job. And then I thought that at the very least, I needed to get out of the middle of the only road around the campground loop, so I carefully, slowly, drove down to the parking lot.

The advantages of being in a crowded place immediately showed up. I had my head under the van for less than five minutes, still trying to figure out what exactly this piece was and how it should be attached when a nice guy wandered over and said, "You need help?"

Yep, I needed help.

He took a look, told me there had to be a piece with a bolt in it somewhere along my path, but that he'd zip tie it up for me in the meantime. I went back to the campsite where I promptly found a long metal rod with a bend at one end and a bolt at the other. By the time I made it back to the parking lot, he'd zip-tied the bracket in place. I showed him the piece and he said he needed to get his trailer set up, but he'd try to come back and help me with it.

I spent the next little while waiting, while also figuring out how the piece worked, where it was supposed to fit, how it needed to go back into place, and trying to get the bolt loose. Basically the bent end of the rod hooked over a hole in an attachment on the frame while the bolt end was attached to the dangling bracket.

I have no idea why it worked its way loose in Yellowstone — I didn't hit anything and I didn't hear anything on the drive — but I theorize that it had come loose from the frame (maybe during the crunch I had in eastern Oregon several weeks ago) and was caught on one of the wires or hoses, and the slope of my campsite was enough to shake it free.

I was starting to think that Helpful Guy #1 must have gotten busy with his own responsibilities and forgotten about me, when Helpful Guy #2 showed up.

I showed him the problem and he went off to his campsite and came back with a set of wrenches. He told me he'd been carrying it around for 15 years and this was the first time he'd ever used it.

I laughed and told him that my collection of tools was always for the last problem I'd had, never for the one I was currently having.

But he loosened the bolt from the rod, and then we put it back into place, he tightened it up for me, and I was good to go.

It was a satisfying outcome to a morning that started out with an unpleasant sinking feeling.

Old Faithful, when I finally got there, did its thing, exactly as expected, among an enormous crowd of people, also as expected. The National Parks really are incredibly popular places.

JUNE 7, 2019 - SOMEWHERE IN NORTH DAKOTA

I will admit the truth: I had very low expectations of North Dakota. I hated South Dakota, which was oppressively hot and windy. I was driving through North Dakota mostly because it was #49 on my lifetime list of states visited and I wanted to get that checkmark on my list.

North Dakota, done.

North Dakota, beautiful? So unexpected!

I spent my first night at a camping spot outside Theodore Roosevelt National Park, windows open, admiring the stars. I would have liked to take the scenic drive all the way around the park, but part of the road was closed. And it was too hot, even early in the day, to drag Z on any long walks. But we paused at the prairie dog town and watched the prairie dogs for a while, then strolled out to a scenic overlook and admired the view. North Dakota and a view. Who knew?

I picked the right time of year to visit North Dakota. I bet South Dakota is nicer in early June than it is at the end of July, too.

JUNE 12, 2019 - MABEL LAKE, MINNESOTA

I was headed to a county park when I passed a national forest campground, Mabel Lake, and swung in to take a look.

It was glorious. Absolutely fantastic dry-camping. For $14, I had a huge site, surrounded by trees, with a short trail that led to an adorable tiny beach.

I could see the water between the trees, but my site was surrounded by gorgeous trees. Trails led into the forest, and it smelled incredible. I don't have the faintest idea what kind of trees they were but every breath felt fresh and clean and... hmm, like Irish Spring soap, actually. Whatever tree Irish Spring smells like, that would be the tree growing in that delightful national forest.

There was only one small problem. Actually, no, there were only about a million small problems.

I like to remind myself when I run into bugs that they are the sign of a healthy ecosystem. That they are essential to the well-being of the planet. That as long as they're not in my space (indoors), I should respect that I'm in their space.

But, OMG, the mosquitoes were insane.

If they'd just been willing to stay outside, I might not have found them so oppressive, but it was impossible to open the door to the van for even a second, without a flood of them pouring inside and going on the attack.

And the thing about mosquitoes, to me, is that I don't actually care that much if they bite me — it itches, so what? — but I hate the sound of them. That high-pitched buzzing in your ear and around your face is so damn annoying.

Mabel Lake was so beautiful and I loved my site so much that on Monday evening, I thought I'd spend a few days there, appreciating the sounds of nature, enjoying solitude and peace. On Tuesday morning, after I walked Zelda while wearing a scarf wrapped around my head and face like a bee-keeper's shroud, I packed up the van and headed out.

JULY 29, 2019 - ALLENTOWN, PENNSYLVANIA

Three years!

If I was going to do justice to this anniversary, I'd add up the numbers: how many campgrounds, how many states, how many miles.

But I don't feel like working that hard. Sometimes it's fun to go through my calendar and make lists, but this past month has been filled with that kind of chore for business reasons and I'm not inspired to do more of it.

I've actually been thinking about this post for months, though. What have I learned in three years of living in a van? What has 50,000 miles of driving taught me?

Mostly that water is precious and that I really don't like driving.

I still miss my house sometimes, although not nearly as much as I miss Bartleby, and I still worry about the future too much.

Before I decided I wasn't going to make lists, I looked through my photos. I was thinking this past year wasn't as busy as the previous two, that I did more adventuring in my first couple years of camping.

Um, no. Not at all. Last summer was upstate New York and Vermont, followed by a delightful couple of months in Canada, then down through Maine and Massachusetts. Florida, then cross-country through Texas and New Mexico to California, and from California, a road trip to Oregon and Idaho, then north to Washington, and cross-country again.

Lots of people, lots of places.

But not enough sunsets. That is, of course, not literally true. We all have exactly the same number of sunsets in a year, after all. But not enough appreciating of sunsets.

Goal for year 4: more time spent appreciating sunsets.

AUGUST 15, 2019 - SOMEWHERE IN MAINE

I came to Maine to meet up with some fellow Travato owners. I arrived a day early, because Gary, an online friend, had offered to teach me to change the oil in my generator. It involved raising the van on ramps, crawling under, draining the old oil, and pumping in the new oil.

Gary did all the hard work, I mostly watched and chatted. Conclusion: yay, I don't need to change the generator oil for another 150 hours or runtime and yay, now I know I will probably not be doing that by myself. Ever.

I paid $125 to have it done the first time it needed doing, which seemed expensive for an oil change, but now I'm thinking was a good deal. Of course, not as good a deal as watching Gary do it!

The rest of the attendees started arriving Friday and continued coming and going throughout the weekend. The spot was beautiful – a house on a hill owned by Trish, a stained glass artist, with incredible art inside, wide porches outside, surrounded by fields of wildflowers, and enough parking room for 20 or so vans to line the driveway.

And the company was delightful — interesting people, doing interesting things, all of us ready to talk about our travels, the places we've enjoyed, adventures on the road, ways of living in our vans and mods. Many, many mods. (AKA modifications to the vans.)

Also, of course, our own lives. On the first day, I wound up sitting with two fellow dog owners, Deb and Ken, talking about journalism, editing, the dot.com years, raising kids with learning disabilities, and writing books. After a couple hours of conversation, Deb said, "Hey, we're going to be on the road for the month of September. If you want our driveway, it's all yours."

I think I probably blinked a few times. Really? They live in Maine, across from a river, with bald eagles living in their trees. I'd been planning to head south, but it was a tempting idea.

That night, everyone brought out our camping chairs and we filled the porches while we ate potluck appetizers and desserts. The next day, some people wandered into town during the morning, while others hung around the house. In the mid-afternoon, Trish collected lobster orders and we all ate corn, grilled vegetables, and fresh Maine lobsters with butter. Afterwards, some people played cards, some played music, and some listened to the music.

The next day was much the same but after dinner, we all carried our chairs out to the firepit in the front lawn and sat around a glorious campfire, toasting marshmallows for s'mores and listening to the musicians sing and play.

On the last day, I bruised my knees. I actually took a picture, which I'm not going to share, because ugh, who wants to look at bruises? But whenever I stumble across it in the future, I'll pat myself on the back.

The story: Trish had warned everyone that animals were welcome but that her dog, Rosey, chased cats and any cats needed to stay in their vans.

On Monday morning, Rosey spotted a cat sitting in the doorway of her van.

It's been a little over a year since Zelda was attacked. Out of nowhere, violence and aggression and blood, and for Zelda, pain and shaky trembling and near-death.

It was traumatic. Afterwards, I became wary of dogs in a way I'd never been before, viscerally aware of how quickly they could do damage, and tense around bigger dogs. I worked on it, though, because I refuse to be scared of dogs.

I think my time in Arcata helped. Sometimes when Suzanne's dog Riley moved quickly or unexpectedly, my heart rate would soar, my breath would catch. He turned out to be the sweetest, softest, loviest dog imaginable, though, which helped me stay present in the fear. Instead of avoiding him and the fear that came with him, I accepted the feeling as just what it was, a feeling.

Desensitization therapy 101.

And that was good, because when Rosey went for the cat, I went for Rosey. Even as I jumped on her, I knew that if she turned around and went for me — a natural reaction for a dog who feels herself being attacked from behind — I was going to get hurt. But I didn't let the fear stop me.

And yay, Rosey didn't go for me, and I didn't get bitten, and the cat escaped and was unhurt and Rosey was unhurt, too. She didn't even get scratched. A couple hours later, she came and snuggled up with me on the porch, letting me give her lots of rubs and scratches, so she didn't hold a grudge either.

I didn't realize I'd landed hard enough to bruise my knees until the next morning, when I rolled out of bed and said, "Ow, what the heck?"

But I'm pleased with those bruises, because they are a symbol of recovery from fear.

I like that in a bruise.

AUGUST 28, 2019 - ALLENTOWN, PENNSYLVANIA

If I could fire myself, I would. I'm such a lousy employee. But what's the saying? On your deathbed, you're never going to regret that you didn't work hard enough? Something like that? I'm never going to regret this delightful last week of summer.

It included video games, mini-golf, playing with the puppy, walking an energetic Zelda, swimming, an outside picnic with burgers on the grill, a quick road trip with my niece to visit my aunt and uncle, looking at old family photos, a trampoline, tetherball, and ice cream.

Actually, lots of ice cream. I think I had ice cream three separate times.

Next stop, back to Maine, for a quiet month of writing. I'm not looking forward to the drive, but very much looking forward to the sitting still time.

AUGUST 30, 2019 - WELLS STATE PARK, MAINE

On Thursday, I started driving to Maine, but instead I drove to Connecticut. And around Connecticut. And more around Connecticut.

Note to self: never take *Serenity* to Connecticut again.

I guess the problem is not "to" Connecticut as much as it is "through" Connecticut. Route 15, aka the Merit Parkway, has bridges that are too low for *Serenity*. Vehicles over 8' are not allowed.

But I couldn't convince either of my GPS systems — Apple Maps on my phone or the GPS in the van — to let me avoid it. I wound up wandering surface streets in random towns and trying not to stress about how much time I was wasting.

Every time I've driven this direction before, I headed north to Albany, NY and then across Massachusetts — a much less direct route — because even people in cars think Connecticut is a nightmare. But

Apple Maps was convinced Connecticut would be faster and I decided I was capable of dealing with traffic, even New York City traffic.

Traffic, yes. Low bridges, no.

I didn't stop until after 1 PM, and by the time I'd finished eating my lunch, traffic had added another hour to my journey. Five more hours to my destination meaning an arrival at 7 PM, not including time for dinner, gas, walking the dog and rush hour traffic.

I decided against. Or rather I decided I would let fate decide. If the state park right next to the highway was full, I'd keep going. If it wasn't, I'd stop for the night. Such a good decision!

Wells State Park isn't universally loved on the camping apps: narrow roads, sloped spaces, no hook-ups or amenities. But it's gorgeous. The host gave me a site "overlooking the water," which is an apt description — I'm high on a hill with a steep slope down to the water, so there's no playing in the water. But the site faces east and the sun is shining on my laptop as I write this, and I'm surrounded by trees and the smells of nature.

Also, plenty of traffic noise, but distant enough that I can pretend it's the sound of the ocean. That is what happens when you aim for a state park right off the highway.

This morning there was an orange note on the van warning me that the town was closing activities between the hours of 6 PM to 8 AM because of the risk of EEE caused by mosquitoes. I was reading this at 7 AM, comfortably within the time of mosquito bite danger, so of course, I walked Zelda feeling paranoid about bugs and itching like mad. But the fog rising off the water as the sun shone on it was so pretty that I enjoyed myself anyway.

SEPTEMBER 19, 2019 - SOUTH GARDINER, MAINE

I looked outside this morning and the fog was so dense that I couldn't see past the middle of the driveway. I thought, "Oooh, how beautiful, I want to go for a walk," and then I paused.

The view from Serenity's window

I've been house-sitting/driveway camping here for over two weeks now. The river has fog every morning, little wisps of it that trickle along the water's surface like ghosts. I've enjoyed watching it but I've noticed that the colder the morning, the more fog there is on the river.

That's not entirely true — there was one crisp, clear, sparkly morning that reminded me of the taste of autumn apples and it wasn't foggy at all. Mostly, though, fog and chill go together.

So before I opened the van door, I asked Alexa for a weather report. 36 degrees! Time to dig out my winter coat. Maybe my upstate New York roots are overcoming the Floridian in me, though — the cold hasn't been bothering me, although I'm not spending as much time sitting outside writing as I imagined I would. That's okay, because the view from the van window is lovely and I like being cozy inside while I write.

By about 7:30, the sun shining through had turned the fog into a mass of gold at the end of the driveway. At 8, it was dancing wisps along the river again. And now, 9:30, it's gone, but all the colors of the day are bright and intense — blues, greens, even the oranges of the leaves in the tree out front.

I read a useful book this week: *Dear Writer, You Need to Quit*, by Becca Syme. I look at a lot of writing books on Amazon, and think, "Maybe someday." This time, I read the Look Inside, purchased the book, then read the book. I'm glad I did.

The book does not actually suggest that one should quit writing, although she does suggest quitting lots of other things, including "Quit Trying to Be Like Everyone Else" and "Quit Focusing on Your Weaknesses." Were those my two favorite chapters? Maybe.

After I finished, I reread *Cici and the Curator*. Cici is the only book of mine that's a comfort reread for me, a story where on a rainy or a sad or a sick day, I read just so I can be part of that other world for a while. She makes me laugh. She still makes me laugh, even though I've read her dozens of times and know every twist — actually every phrase! — inside and out. And sure, I get critical the way I do with my other books — clunky line, repetition, a little slow here — the editor brain never shuts off. But not in a way that ruins my enjoyment.

Cici has sold fewer than 300 copies, and earned considerably less than $1000. From a business point of view, it makes no sense to write more books like *Cici*. But *Cici* brings me joy. And you know, life is better when you focus on what brings you joy and not on what earns you money.

Obviously, starvation, homelessness, pain and suffering are all not likely to bring me joy, so I'd like to avoid total penury. But for the moment I'm going to accept the permission to quit trying to be like everyone else (not that I ever tried very hard, to be honest) and write what brings me joy.

SEPTEMBER 23, 2019 - SOUTH GARDINER, MAINE

I'm loving Maine. It's crazily beautiful where I am. The night sky is so gorgeous — lots of stars to see, not hidden behind light pollution. I even saw a shooting star Saturday night, which always feels special.

The leaves are falling now and when the wind blows, they skitter across the pavement. The trees across the river that were a block of green three weeks ago are now scattered with color — still mostly green but with bursts of deep red and yellow, scarlet and bright orange.

I didn't kayak as much as I would have liked, mostly because I was actually working hard. So unusual!

The light at sunrise is so beautiful. The moment when the sun crests the hill of trees, directly across the river from the van window, and the light reaches the water is a true moment. Not the slow change from night to day, not the slow lightening of the sky, but a specific two minute period where suddenly the van is golden and the leaves of the trees are outlined in color, a translucent bright green instead of the usual mass.

The color of the light is different than at any other time. It's not that it's brighter, I don't think — and actually the shadows are very long, so no, it's not brighter. It's a contrast between darkness and brightness, a glow. And the fog usually has its ghost tendrils dancing on the water, but they are still in shadow, so the trees and lawn are bright and green and golden, but just beyond them is misty shadowed gloom. Yeah, it's cool as anything, and truly beautiful.

OCTOBER 7, 2019 - ALLENTOWN, PENNSYLVANIA

On this relatively bleak Monday morning — gray and gloomy, and the kind of day where putting the spoons away includes bumping my head on the counter, and reaching for the coffee means spilling tea everywhere — I'm reminding myself to breathe and be grateful.

Breathe and be grateful. Pretty much the two best pieces of advice ever.

So what am I grateful for? Well, I'm grateful that there are no signs of a leak to go with the continuously running water pump. That's a good thing.

I'm grateful that even though my battery seems to have mysteriously depleted its charge in the night well past recommended levels, it still seems to work (witness the continuously running water pump.)

I'm grateful that even though the tank level monitor appears to be completely screwed up, I never really used it much anyway.

I'm grateful that the stomach flu that had me miserable throughout Saturday night and most of Sunday was short-lived. Yay to eating solid food again.

I'm grateful that my roof isn't leaking in the rain, I'm grateful that it's warm enough that even though I've run out of propane, I'm not uncomfortable. Oh, and it occurs to me that maybe I haven't run out of propane, maybe I'm just relying on a tank level monitor that's screwed up at the moment, ha.

I'm grateful that Zelda is snoring at my feet and ate breakfast this morning and that we went for a good walk in the dark before 6AM, because I was feeling better and she was lively.

I'm grateful that even though I didn't make it to the Shenandoah National Park, I'm parked in a comfortable street. And that even though the weather is not lovely, it's not lousy either, just somewhere in between.

So much to be grateful for!

And yet, somehow, it's still a struggle...

OCTOBER 11, 2019 - LITTLE FORT CAMPGROUND, THE GEORGE WASHINGTON NATIONAL FOREST

When I started driving south, my plan was to take it slow, seeing the scenery along the way. I had my sights on a small National Forest campground for my first night, to be followed by a drive through Shenandoah, then more driving along the Blue Ridge Parkway with overnight stops as needed.

By the weekend, North Carolina. I'd explore Asheville and the Great Smoky Mountains, and maybe check out the ruby mine in Cherokee, because I liked the sapphire mine so much.

In other words, I'd be a tourist.

The only problem with that plan is that I actually want to work instead. I want to finish the book I'm writing.

My first destination is a tiny campground, only nine sites, with no amenities. No water, no hook-ups, no showers, no dump station, no garbage service. Also no internet access and no cell service. It's also free, so you know, you get what you pay for.

Except not really, because it is beautiful and treed and peaceful. Not a view, exactly — it's just a spot in the middle of a forest — but out of every window I see trees, just starting to pick up their autumn color.

The campground seems to be a base point for people with ATVs, so occasionally the noise of humankind is loud. But mostly it's crickets. Literal crickets, lots and lots of them. At night, the only lights I can see are the ones created by the van and by nature. And once a campfire from people across the way.

I feel like I should see the National Parks, since I'm so close. And I think I should take the long scenic drives, and admire the beauty of the autumn countryside. And I think I should explore Asheville, a town I've been told I'll love.

But what I want to do is finish writing my book. So for the past two days, I've played with words and stared into space and eaten nice food and taken occasional walks with Z and enjoyed my life.

Ever so much, enjoyed my life.

Camping in North Carolina

OCTOBER 17, 2019 - PISGAH NATIONAL FOREST, NORTH CAROLINA

On Monday, I was meandering toward Asheville and stopped at a Salvation Army store to do a little shopping. I managed to replace the jeans that developed holes in the knees a few weeks ago, plus picked up a cotton sweater to add to my warm weather layer collection.

I also had a pleasant chat with a woman in the parking lot, who was impressed that I was traveling by myself.

She wanted to know if I carried a weapon with me.

I do not.

She shook her head and eyed the van, and told me I was very brave.

I told her that my weapon was my car keys: if I ever felt unsafe, I just drove away.

Isn't it strange how life provides its own foreshadowing sometimes?

Later in the day, I headed up into the hills of Pisgah National Forest to the Curtis Creek campground. The drive was up a winding narrow dirt road with multiple one-lane bridges — the kind of road that made me wonder what I was getting myself into.

The campground sites were clustered together in a small meadow. I kept driving, hoping to find a spot that was more secluded and suddenly I was out of the campground, still climbing into the mountains.

But the road was narrow and there wasn't an easy place to turn around. As I drove, I passed a couple of parked cars with tents set up in the woods nearby. I realized they were dispersed camping, which is the term for camping in the national forests outside a designated campground.

After several minutes of driving, I found a spot in the road wide enough to easily turn *Serenity*. Instead, I parked and ate a late lunch and considered dispersed camping.

I hadn't done it before and it felt spooky. It was so isolated. I was alone in the forest. No neighbors, no one around at all. And I had no cell service, of course, nor internet.

It was a beautiful forest, though. Lots of green and a bit of autumn color. I could hear running water from a nearby brook and birds chirping. Z and I went for a cautious walk while I thought about bears and broken ankles and the amazing beauty of real nature.

And then we came back to *Serenity* and settled in. I opened the windows, and started reading my book, and Z snuggled up and went to sleep.

As it got dark, I listened to the sound of the brook and appreciated the chilly fresh air while a full moon started to rise. Then, of course, I thought about werewolves, and wished I hadn't read so many shapeshifter books that start with a woman being attacked in a remote forest. The light from the moon was so bright that twice I checked to be sure I hadn't left the outside light on.

In the morning, I was feeling ever so cheerful and optimistic. I'd had a restless night, but my free campsite in the woods felt like a fine place to spend the day. Totally isolated. I'd get out the computer and do nothing but think about my book until I was finished.

And then I heard a car pull up and stop right next to me.

Huh.

That was odd.

A ranger? I didn't think I needed a permit for dispersed camping, but maybe I did. The car was behind the van, so I opened the bathroom door to look out the back window.

It was not a car, it was a pickup truck.

And it was not a ranger.

The guy who'd gotten out of the truck was scruffy, pudgy, dressed in camouflage. He was behind the hood of the truck and he was doing something that I couldn't quite see.

But — and this was clearly paranoia — it looked like he was loading a gun.

I watched him for several seconds that felt like minutes. Maybe hours.

Okay, yes, he was loading a gun.

That was not paranoia.

That was what he was doing.

In this totally isolated spot in the forest, a strange man had parked behind my van and was loading a gun.

I glanced back into the van. I had a bunch of kitchen stuff out. Olive oil, dishes, hot water on the stove for making coffee. How fast could I safely put things away? Should I put things away? How fast could I get moving? If I grabbed the keys and jumped into the driver's seat...

My brain was racing almost as fast as my heart was pounding.

Then I heard a car door slam. I looked at the pickup truck again, and nothing had changed. No one else was there, just the guy with his gun. So I scooted over to the front of the van and yanked open the curtain that separates the seats from the kitchen.

Another pickup truck was parked in front of me. Two men were getting out. Both of them were carrying guns, too.

And neither of them was scary, because they were both wearing bright orange baseball caps on top of their camouflage.

Hunters.

Guess what October 15th probably is in North Carolina? I say probably because I don't know for sure, not having had internet access, but I'm going to guess that it's the opening day of a hunting season.

Because for the next twenty minutes, while I packed up the van and got ready to go, truck after truck after truck drove up my remote, isolated, completely secluded, private forest road, carrying guys, guns, and dogs. Lots of dogs.

Also more men with guns than I have ever seen in my life.

It was a party. A gun-toting, animal-hunting, celebration-of-fall party.

By 9AM, I was on the road, driving cautiously to avoid hitting pickup trucks on the one-lane bridges. So many trucks, so many people.

So not the glorious day of isolated writing in a beautiful spot that I was anticipating.

PART III

9

HOW IT ENDED

The very beloved dog turned 15 this week. She got liver treats for her birthday and ate them eagerly. I'm always happy when she eats eagerly — it doesn't happen often.

We still go for walks, we still snuggle, she still plays with her toys. She doesn't respond to voice commands anymore, or only rarely. That's the canine dementia in action. But she knows her hand signals and follows them without hesitation.

Her eyes are still bright, she is still curious. She snores now, though, which she didn't use to, and I rather love it. It's not a big snore, just a sweet snore.

Sometimes I lie awake and listen to her breathe, and dread the day that the van falls silent. That silence is going to hurt. But it's not silent yet and it reminds me to appreciate every day I get with her. I've had a lot more of them than I expected to have in May 2018, so I'm counting my blessings.

I am so lucky. And she is so beloved.

JANUARY 29, 2020 - SANFORD, FLORIDA

I took a business trip today, the kind of business trip you get to take when you're a writer. I drove to the Ocala National Forest with two terrific companions (Z and R) and took a nice hike along a wilderness trail, located at my imagined site for the fictional town of Tassamara.

It was a search for inspiration.

Sadly, I can't say that I was inspired. But I did have a nice time.

Yesterday R and I went out to lunch at what used to be our favorite sushi restaurant in Winter Park. It was fantastic. I think I'd almost forgotten how good really good sushi can be. On the way home, we drove by our old house, just to look at it. The new owner (not really new anymore) has painted it a much more sedate color — a gray blue, with a red door — and changed some of the landscaping.

I was glad because the pang of loss was a lot less intense than the last time I saw it. I didn't love it anymore. As we drove away, I realized that even though I've missed my house many times in the past years, I wouldn't go back, even if I could.

It was a good house for what I needed at the time, but it's not what I need anymore or even what I want. I'm always going to remember my back porch and my kitchen with nostalgic pleasure, though.

FEBRUARY 18, 2020 - SANFORD, FLORIDA

On Valentine's Day, I went grocery shopping with Christina and Frisbee. On the way into the store, I said, "Oh, yay, Valentine's Day. I shall buy myself some chocolate."

Thus ensued a brief conversation about Hallmark holidays, which Christina scorns. Years ago, I too hated Valentine's Day. It's such a loaded holiday for anyone not happily partnered. These days, though, I like all holidays that can be labeled chocolate holidays, because they're an excuse to eat chocolate, and I like reasons to eat chocolate.

Christina pointed out that I can have chocolate whenever I want, and I said, sure, but if I ate chocolate every day it wouldn't be special.

I view chocolate holidays as a reason to check in with myself. I'm the person who takes care of me, so I'm the one who gets to say, "Hmm, would flowers make me happy today?" And if they would, I buy myself some flowers.

And yes, I could potentially do this every day, but I can't afford flowers every day, or chocolate every day. Even if I could, it would then just become routine. Things you take for granted don't make you happy. Things you appreciate, do.

Anyway, I went into the grocery store with every intention of buying some chocolate. Sadly, the grocery store had no chocolate without the wheat warning label. None!

I read the label on every chocolate bar they had. Before I was done, Christina was also reading labels. But there was no safe chocolate.

So it goes. I bought myself some gluten-free bagels, smoked salmon and cream cheese, because hey, just because I couldn't have chocolate didn't mean I couldn't have a treat. I toasted my bagel in Christina's toaster and it was delicious. Treat success.

The next day Christina and Frisbee went out to lunch, and came back with gluten-free Thin Mint-style cookies (which tasted exactly like Thin Mints) and a gluten-safe chocolate bar for me.

And you know, treats you buy yourself are great, but treats from thoughtful friends are even better. I finished my chocolate bar last night and fell asleep feeling loved. It's amazing what a little chocolate can do.

MARCH 3, 2020 - SANFORD, FLORIDA

I'm starting to look at maps and campground apps. In a week or so, I'll be on the road again, making my way across the country.

My last cross-country drive was in the north, through Montana and Minnesota, but I'm early enough this year that I'm going to stick to the south to avoid the cold. But I might zoom through the east to Texas, then slow down and enjoy the wildflowers for a while. I don't need to be in a hurry.

My ultimate goal, though, is Arcata. I'm going to spend a month or so there and help Suzanne with the chores we didn't get to last year, plus have a delicious gluten-free cupcake on my birthday and take Zelda to the beach, then spend the summer exploring Oregon and the Pacific Northwest. Maybe even Glacier, which I've been hoping to get to for years.

It's been absurdly hot, so hot I woke up yesterday morning and immediately turned the air-conditioning on. And humid, too. It feels like living in the tropics, which I ought to love — and sort of do — but living in a metal box in 90 degree weather is not nearly as much fun as living in a metal box in 70 degree weather.

But I decided to set my departure date by the weather report. Like Mary Poppins, when the wind changes...

It might be a weird time to travel, though. Last night, I couldn't fall asleep. My throat hurt, my nose was running, and I wondered whether I was coming down with something.

I reassured myself that it couldn't possibly be the corona virus and then remembered that two of the people I've been spending time with, Frisbee and Max, flew through international airports within the past month. Plus, they've visited Disney and Universal Studios. They could totally have given me germs. Of course, it's far more likely that I'm having a gluten reaction.

MARCH 11, 2020 - DESOTO NATIONAL FOREST

Today was a long driving day, which unfortunately for me meant a lot of time swinging back and forth between ruminating and worrying.

And then pausing somewhere in the middle of the swing to remind myself to breathe, to live in the present, to admire the scenery and enjoy the experience.

Worrying and ruminating, both, are just choosing to spend time in my own negative brain instead of choosing to be in my real world's current pleasant experience.

Sure, COVID-19 may become an exponential disaster next week, but it's not like I can do anything about that. Except maybe relocate some of the plastic gloves that I carry for dumping the tanks to the door of the van, so when I pump gas, I remember not to touch the gas handle with bare skin.

Still, I made great progress in my driving and managed to get to a rather nice parking lot. I can't call it a campground — I'm not sure what's required to turn empty land into a campground, but something is. A clear demarkation of campsites, maybe? Fire rings? Whatever is needed, this place lacks it. It's a parking lot.

But a nice parking lot in a national forest.

MARCH 13, 2020 - LOUISIANA TO TEXAS

If I could have seen three days into the future on Monday, I suspect I would have said, "Florida, what a lovely place to hang out, despite the heat. I believe I'll stick around."

But I couldn't see into the future and even though I did anticipate that the corona virus situation might keep getting crazier, I kinda thought it would take a few weeks.

Wow, what a difference three days can make.

Not that anything is particularly different in my life. I'm not sick and the highways still have plenty of cars driving on them.

And the grocery stores still have plenty of people. It does seem strange that everyone said, "Hey, pandemic, let's go shopping," but I guess that will taper off once everyone starts hunkering down.

Speaking of hunkering down, it's not easy to hunker down in a van. I can't stock up for two weeks of self-imposed quarantine, much less the decade the people buying all the toilet paper seem to be planning for.

On Tuesday, I decided I'd stay at my trailhead for another night and settled in with my book. Then I tried to cook some rice and realized my propane wasn't working. Before I panicked, I checked the tank level and discovered it was empty.

Poor planning on my part, but it meant it was time to get on the road. I packed up, started driving, found myself a dump station, some propane, some gas, and some fresh salad greens, and finally a comfortable rest stop in Louisiana (the Atchafalaya Welcome Center) to spend the night.

In the morning, the propane still didn't work. Argh! I was super annoyed — the last time I went off-grid it didn't work, and I was going to get it looked at, but then it started working again, so I didn't. Things that work erratically are so frustrating.

But then I could hear my mom's voice in my head, saying, "If that's the worst that happens..."

We're in the middle of a pandemic and apparent economic collapse, so I think I can manage without a working stove. The (obnoxiously loud) generator works, so I can still cook, just not quietly.

That afternoon, I stopped at a county park, Whites Park in Wallisville, Texas.

It's strange. There are no signs, no ranger station, no place to check in, no visible instructions anywhere — just grass and trees and some posts that look like they should mark a row of campsites. I would hate it if it was filled with people: the posts are close together, lined up in a row, parking lot style.

But it's not filled with people. In fact, I was the only camper there. I drove around the park, puzzled by my solitude, then pulled over and read the reviews again. The first review said, "I might not camp here if I were a woman camping alone, but I feel totally safe with my partner with me."

Hmm...

I did feel safe, though. It was empty, but not scary. Also, there was water so I could fill my tanks. Also, lots of grass for Z to hang out on. I took my version of reasonable precautions, so when I went to sleep, everything was packed and ready to go, nothing left outside, all storage latched and ready. If necessary, I could have hopped out of bed, turned the key in the ignition and been gone. I'm glad it wasn't necessary.

I wanted to see wildflowers in Texas, but this patch at a rest stop was the closest I came.

MARCH 15, 2020 - GUADALUPE RIVER STATE PARK

I started coughing in Houston.

I told myself it was seasonal allergies, but I upped my social distancing as much as possible: I wore disposable gloves at the gas station when pumping gas and using the touch pad; shoved doors open with my feet; used hand sanitizer liberally; stood several feet away from the campground host; and touched nothing at the ranger station.

Obviously, that was probably the "too little, too late," that the shutdowns are meant to stop. If I'd known I was getting sick, I wouldn't be on the road, but I am on the road and there's not a lot I can do about it.

At the moment, I'm in Guadalupe River State Park. I believe there's a scenic overlook within easy walking distance, but I haven't seen it, because easy walking distance is not feeling easy. Not that I'm that sick — I feel like I've got a cold. In normal times, I'd take some cold medicine and make myself some soup and get over it. In these non-normal times, I'll probably do the same.

Yesterday, when I was still feeling like maybe I was just allergic, I cooked all the things: rice, quinoa, chicken, steak, salmon. My goal was to make enough food that I could eat quinoa or rice bowls with protein and greens for the next several days and not worry about needing the stove or electricity. Today that's feeling rather convenient.

Also nice: my ample supply of HEB spice gum drops (the best spice gum drops ever). I didn't plan on eating them while sitting still — they're meant to be a treat for long driving days, but I'm enjoying them. It's probably not the healthiest choice, but carpe diem for spice gum drops. I'm sure the cinnamon ones are good for me.

MARCH 19, 2020 - THE MIDDLE OF NOWHERE, ARIZONA

"Our worries are just there to make ourselves miserable but our finger is on the button: we can stop worrying." - *The Big Leap*, Gay Hendricks

I read that book in January. Ha. Would that it were so easy!

I left Guadalupe River on Monday. First, though, I was obsessive about my germs. I wiped down the faucet, the water spigot, and the electricity post with my precious antiseptic wipes, trying to make sure every surface I'd even come close to was smothered in bleach. If someone arrived soon after I departed, there might still have been white cleaning suds on the faucet, but the germs would definitely have been dead.

At least as long as they were of the 99.9% killed by antiseptic wipes.

I have no way to know whether I have covid or a cold — I'm not sick enough to require testing nor rich enough to get randomly tested the way the celebrities seem to be doing — but I was definitely not healthy enough to drive for endless hours.

I made it to the New Mexico border, spent a miserable night at a rest stop; made it to Arizona, spent a more pleasant night at Saddle River; made it to the Arizona/California border and said, yeah, done. I checked my apps for the closest Bureau of Land Management area, drove into the desert, parked and went to sleep.

I've been careful along the way. I used my nitrile gloves and antiseptic wipes at every gas station, and I'm living on the food I have in my fridge. I haven't spoken to another person (except on the phone) in days.

But this is definitely not a good time to be living in a van.

Also, not a great time for the propane not to be functioning. No propane and no electricity means no heat. Is this ironic, given that I left Florida because it was getting too hot or just an unpleasant coincidence?

It's also not a great time to be sick. Yesterday I was running a fever and coughing. I didn't feel like I needed a doctor, though. I was just sick enough to stay in bed. I'm hoping that turns into healthy enough to get back on the road soon. Meanwhile, I'm hanging out in the desert.

MARCH 20, 2020 - SOMEWHERE IN ARIZONA

My "middle of nowhere" site in the desert is in the middle of nowhere, as far I'm concerned. It's not a real campground and there's not a building within sight, although there are lights on the horizon at night.

But I stayed close to the road, and cars or trucks drive by at least once an hour during the daylight hours. Plus, at least half a dozen other RVs or campers are within sight, although several hundred feet away. Close enough that I know my nearest neighbors were running their generator at 2 AM, which is probably close enough that if I desperately needed help, I could stumble my way to their camper and cough on them. I assume they'd call for help then, because campers are usually nice people.

The middle of nowhere

That said, I did spend a while in the dark of the night last night, when my fever was back, wondering whether we were apocalyptic enough that someone finding me delirious in the camper would kick me out to die in the desert before stealing the van.

Survival of the fittest, after all, and I've never believed I'd be a survivor in any apocalyptic scenario. I lack the killer instinct. I'm not even willing to stock up on toilet paper, lest the next person need it more than I do.

In the bright light of day, however, my fever is gone (again!), and I think I'm getting better (again!). Whatever I have, it's weird, because it seems to come and go in waves.

Some of it is exhaustion: I use up my energy and then I'm just completely depleted, to the level of lie on the bed, cry and feel sorry for myself. Sick enough I can't even read because I can't focus. And then a few hours later, I think I'm on the mend again.

Still, at this exact moment in time, I can practice happiness. I'm admiring a beautiful sky, there's a lovely cool breeze, my avocado was perfect, and I can listen to music. My life is good and I'm grateful. Also ready to feel healthy again, but anticipating it will happen any day now.

MARCH 23, 2020 - QUARTZITE, ARIZONA

On Friday, I backtracked twenty miles or so to Quartzite, Arizona.

It was mostly to make my brother happy. He was sending me map views of my location from the data in my photographs, linking me to local hospital information, and muttering (as much as one can mutter in a text) about police and wellness checks in the desert. Moving to Quartzite meant meeting up with several members of a Facebook group for solo travelers, i.e., people to call the ambulance if necessary. It has not been necessary. Yay!

It's weird, though. We're social distancing to the max, so apart from one brief hello from about twenty-five feet away, I haven't met my fellow solo travelers. I'd love to talk to them, but instead I wave from the van window if I see them moving around outside. So it goes.

It also feels weird to just be sitting here. I keep trying to remind myself that this is real life. I should be writing a book. I should be — I don't know, lots of things.

Instead, I'm obsessively checking the news and Facebook as if something's going to be different from the last time I looked. I remind myself to breathe and meditate and listen to music and before I can do anything of the sort, I just need one last look at the *Washington Post*. And then an hour has gone by and I remind myself that I could be meditating, which lasts five minutes before I think maybe a quick glance at Facebook will do something other than annoy me.

I'm almost always wrong about that.

A while back I was working on a post-apocalyptic story called "Welcome to tH3-3ND," where a virus (H3-3ND) decimated the world. I gave up on it, because I felt like I needed to know more about infrastructure to do it justice, but the thing I got very, very wrong is the tedium of the minute-by-minute indecision.

Real life is suspended, but what gets put in its place? I've never understood stories with people who leave their shelters in the zombie apocalypse, but now I do.

Socially distanced camper vans

MARCH 26, 2020 - SOMEWHERE IN CALIFORNIA

Random thought: Thank God for Dairy Queen, La Quinta, and Quality Inn, because otherwise the alphabet game (the one where you find letters on signs and license plates) would be well-nigh impossible. Also much appreciation to all the lawyers who post billboards that start with "Injured?" because that J comes in handy.

Why, after three and a half years of driving around the country, I decided to start playing the alphabet game, I don't know. But I've played it for hours and hours and hours, and I would now like to never play it again. I did get good at it, though. My fastest game was about 2 minutes in the San Jose area; my slowest was about 5 hours across the Arizona desert. Pro tip: J and Q are the hard letters, while X and V are surprisingly easy because of Exits and Vehicles.

Next random thought: I prefer positive gratitudes to negative gratitudes. And if our vocabulary had better emotional granularity, we would have two words for the feeling of gratitude; one for the happy, content gratitude inspired by a cup of coffee or some beautiful flowers — the gratitude of small delights — and another for the resigned gratitude of, "At least it isn't worse."

I've had a lot of the latter gratitude: I'm grateful not to be worrying about feeding six children; I'm grateful not to be in an ICU struggling to breathe.

But I highly, highly recommend not living in a van during a pandemic. Just FYI.

Moving on to some actual story: On Monday, I decided I was healthy enough to look for someone to fix my propane. I thought it would take a few days to get an appointment or I would discover it was impossible, depending on how Arizona was handling non-essential needs.

As it happened, the second person I called was willing to take a look that afternoon, if I could meet him in between jobs. I warned him that I'd been sick, but was feeling better, and we agreed to practice excellent social distancing.

About three hours later, the propane was fixed, more or less.

Post propane-success, I decided to tackle the water issue. I have four gallon jugs for drinking water, plus the tank on the van for water for washing and flushing. Three jugs were empty and the tank was down to $1/4$ full.

I could have (should have!) stopped at the RV Pit Stop in Quartzite before I left to fill up, but at the time I was focused on the propane and it didn't occur to me. Water felt like an easy problem to solve.

Two closed campgrounds and three stores with empty shelves later, with one measly half-gallon jug to show for my labors, it felt rather more critical.

Human beings need close to a gallon of water a day. This is an imperative, not optional. We can survive without electricity, we can survive without internet, we can survive without a cell signal, but we can't survive without a supply of clean, drinkable water.

But we take it so much for granted in this country. We just don't worry about where our clean water will come from.

Until we're homeless, I guess, or living in a van during a pandemic.

With my water supply running low and campgrounds closed or closing, I was torn: back to Quartzite to restock and socially distance with the other solo travelers? It was already warm and Arizona gets hot fast. Within the week, average temperatures would be in the mid-80s, which would not be fun with no possibility of shade and no electricity hook-up.

Or continue on to Arcata? And if Arcata, how to go? Leisurely, up through Nevada, stopping often, and waiting out the weather if there was snow in the mountains, or the most direct route, which would take me through the San Francisco Bay Area?

I think the empty shelves in the grocery stores supplied my answer. I understand the logical reasons why the shelves are both empty now and won't be empty for long, but it's still anxiety-provoking to see that all the rice except for the arborio is gone, ditto all the Campbell's canned soup. Only mildly, since I like Arborio rice and can't eat most soup, but it doesn't feel like a good time to be traveling.

Straight to Arcata it was.

By 9 PM, I was across the border and settling down for the night at the campground at Chiriaco Summit. The campground had no amenities, just a row of nicely spaced campsites, but it was also free.

By 7:30 AM, I was back on the road. I told myself I'd write morning words and check my email at a rest stop. But instead I drove. And drove. And drove.

I was not alone. For plenty of the time, I wondered who all the other people on the road with me were and why they weren't staying home.

All the highway alert signs said something like, "Avoid Travel, Stay

At Home to Stop COVID-19" and every time I saw one I felt guilty, but at least I was actually in my home, even if it was moving.

When I got to Oakland, though — familiar territory to me, because I used to live there — it became obvious how actually empty the roads were. I think I drove through Oakland-Berkeley in about 10 minutes, never going below 60MPH and that's just unthinkable. It definitely felt surreal.

MARCH 26, 2020 - ARCATA, CALIFORNIA

After Oakland, my ETA for arrival in Arcata was still before 9 PM, if just barely.

It would have been an exhaustingly long driving day — over 800 miles and more than 12 hours behind the wheel, but the thought of a real shower was pushing me onward.

Let's pause and discuss showers for a minute. I'm going to admit a horrifying truth: because I was worried about spreading germs in public bathrooms and because my propane didn't work so I had no hot water and then because I didn't have any water, I haven't taken a real shower since leaving Florida. Wet washcloth and shower wipes, and that's it.

To say I'm feeling grimy would be like saying the Titanic was a small boat. Most of it is psychological, really. Shower wipes work quite well and there are people advocating for never washing your hair who have gone years without shampoo. I don't think anyone would look at me (or smell me) and know how long it's been since I felt clean. Still, psychological grime is still grime, and two and a half weeks is a long time to go without washing. I wanted a shower!

But when I stopped in Willets for my third tank of gas, I had a text from Suzanne: the nurse next door wanted us to be safe, so I would need to isolate when I got to Arcata.

Also, the driveway I was planning to park in is under repair and was going to need another month plus before being usable.

It would be street parking and no shower for me.

Like that, my motivation to keep driving disappeared in a puff of exhaustion.

But campgrounds are non-essential and all non-essential businesses in California are closed. Hotels are non-essential, too. I spent at least fifteen minutes on the phone with an irrepressibly perky customer service agent who was sure she could find me a room somewhere before saying apologetically, "Um, I think all our hotels are closed."

Yeah, that's what I thought, too. So no hotel, no shower; no campsite with water and electricity. Also no overnight parking in rest stops. And no overnight parking at Walmarts.

It was not my finest moment of van life.

But there was a Bureau of Land Management campground about 45 minutes back in the direction from which I'd come.

Was I happy to be driving 45 minutes in the wrong direction? Nope. I was even less happy when 30 minutes later Apple Maps tried to send me down a road heavily signposted with "No exit, no turn around, do not use," signs.

I gazed at the signs for a solid couple of minutes, considering my options. Did I want to take my chances? Answer: no. With a sigh, I pulled up my camping apps again, found the next camping area that seemed like it might be open and started driving, still in the wrong direction.

In the wrong direction and up the kind of narrow, winding, bumpy road that makes for an exciting start to an adventure. At least it does at 9 AM on a weekend, when you're going camping with friends and the sun is shining and venturing into the unknown is part of the thrill.

At 7:45 PM on a cold and rainy night, when the sun is setting and it's getting dark and you've been driving for 12 hours, it's not so fun.

I drove and I drove, and every possible pull-off spot had a No Camping sign plastered on a nearby tree. By 8:20 PM, when it was full dark, completely black, I was driving about five miles per hour because I couldn't see a thing. The GPS said my potential campground was still 3 miles away.

I said, "The hell with it."

I pulled over in a No Camping spot, turned off the van, and crawled into my bed. I think I was asleep ten minutes later.

At 11:30 I woke up and spent the next two hours imagining plaintive conversations with the police. Eventually, I fell asleep again and fortunately, no police officers ever showed up to send me on my way.

In the morning, while I was still lying in bed, I watched two deer delicately stepping their way past the van down the road. It was a reminder of the positive side of van life. And the forest I was surrounded by was quite beautiful. Also cold and foggy, but in an appealingly gothic way.

A good setting for a murder mystery.

I considered finding the campground I'd been looking for and settling in. Sadly, I still hadn't resolved my water problem so any settling in would have been short-term. Instead I got back on the road, drove a leisurely three or four hours, and made it to Arcata in time for Suzanne to feed me avocado toast, sushi, blackberries and a GF chocolate chip cookie for dinner.

From a safe distance, of course.

We discussed — also from a safe distance — the proper isolating timeline. We settled on another three days without fever for me, which conveniently times the end of my isolation to her first day off. Obviously, if my fever comes back, the timeline changes, but except for a case of the sniffles — allergies, in my opinion — and the natural tired from some long driving days, I feel okay.

I'm not sure how long it will work for me to camp in her street, though. Driveway camping can be comfortable, but street camping is exhausting. People walking by, cars driving by... On a quiet street, it can be okay, but on a busy street — like this one — it's much worse than parking lot camping. But I'm going to take it one day at a time.

Today the sun is shining, the van is warm thanks to my working propane heater, my dog is happy, and I have some writing to do.

APRIL 8, 2020 - ARCATA, CALIFORNIA

Yesterday was my birthday and I managed to have a really nice day, despite the end of the world busily happening. Mostly because Suzanne rocked the "giving your friend a good birthday" skill.

The cupcake store is closed, but is doing special orders, which meant I couldn't get a single gluten-free cupcake, but I could get a dozen of them. Carpe diem! I'm sharing, but I've still eaten three.

But after yesterday's first cupcake, we went to the beach. An isolated, northern California style beach — the closest we came to other human beings was well within the social distancing 6 feet and probably closer to the realistic 22 feet that airborne pathogens can spread from a cough or sneeze.

We brought all three dogs and I let Zelda off leash, which I don't usually do these days since she a) can't hear and b) can be quite forgetful, including forgetting she's supposed to stay near her people. But it was a big empty beach with plenty of room for her to run around within my line of view. She had a wonderful time.

She's so tired today that when I went in the house for lunch I couldn't even convince her to raise her head off the bed, much less accompany me, but I'm sure she would say it was worth it.

After a couple hours at the beach, we came back to the house and while I spent some time on the phone, Suzanne picked up take-out sushi we'd pre-ordered from a local restaurant. She built a fire in the backyard fire pit and we ate fireside.

Afterwards, we toasted Peeps and marshmallows over the fire. We sat and chatted until the sun went down and the colorful solar lanterns lit up and the fire turned to coals, then embers, then ashes. All three dogs stayed close and Tank, the supposedly feral black cat, came and sat in my lap and purred at me for a while.

In between the beach and the fire, I checked my email and I had the loveliest email from a reader. It was such icing on the cake of a nice day. I know I haven't done a good job of marketing my last book — my March goal was to rewrite the description, and I didn't even manage that — but writing has been so bad for me in the last year that I've questioned why I even bother. But L wrote, "your books never fail to make my days better." That's worth writing for.

I read Suzanne the entire email and she told me to print it, frame it, and hang it on my wall, and if I had a wall, I actually might. Vans don't have a lot of wall space, though.

APRIL 14, 2020 - ARCATA, CALIFORNIA

The weather is warming up, which means it was 48 instead of 44 when I went on my morning walk with Zelda, and it might hit 62 this afternoon. I'm not complaining, though, because I know how hot it is in Florida and how miserable we would be if we were living there while it was 95 degrees.

Zelda loves this weather. She's always eager to walk. I keep threatening her with a harness because she wants to run and I don't like being dragged. Yep, my fifteen year old dog is dragging me down the street. That's good news.

I have no other news. I'm social-isolating like a good pandemic survivor. Unfortunately, isolation offers a lot of time for self-reflection. In the grand scheme of things, self-reflection is close to infinitely more worthwhile than reading the news, following social media, or watching the death toll tick up on the *Washington Post* map tracker, but I'm sick of it nonetheless. The line between insight and insult is too easy for me to cross.

Yesterday Suzanne and I took the dogs to the park after dinner and while we were there, she said, "That dinner was so good." Then she laughed and said, "Is that the fourth time I've said that?"

Yep.

It made me laugh, though, because dinner was grilled cheese sandwiches and soup. So exciting, yes? Admittedly, the grilled cheese sandwiches were made with caramelized onions, and the soup was sweet potato with ginger, smoked paprika, brown rice and spinach, so, yeah, it was good.

The relevance is that whenever the level of self-insult rises too high, at least I can remind myself that I taught myself to cook.

And making a fantastic grilled cheese sandwich is not the world's least accomplishment.

APRIL 25, 2020 - ARCATA, CALIFORNIA

When I was in Arcata, a year — or maybe a lifetime? — ago, Suzanne's stepson, J, was living in her backyard, in a building known as the Tiniest House. It's the former garage, sorta remodeled for habitability. The garage door is gone, replaced by a wall, and the ceiling is sloped, with skylights.

But I say "sorta" because while it has a bathroom, it didn't (apparently) have hot water. While it has nice laminate flooring, they mistakenly installed the flooring without putting a moisture guard between it and the ground, so it needs to be redone. There's a tiny kitchen area, but the countertop is unfinished and the cabinets have no doors, with the plumbing open to the room. There was no heat and the electricity was unchanged since maybe the 1950s. And the walls are bright orange and green, and by bright, I mean glaring.

J was talking about moving out. I claimed first dibs, if and when he did.

It was theoretical. Maybe a plan for when I got tired of traveling, a few years in the future. Maybe a plan for when Suzanne retired, several years in the future. Maybe a plan for when one or both of us had enough money to really fix up the place.

Or, you know, maybe a plan for when the world is having a major pandemic and I'm trying to live in a street. That could be the right time, too.

So, yeah, plans for fixing up the Tiniest House have been occupying much of my attention and internet time recently. We started with the electricity: it's now been inspected and confirmed safe by an actual electrician and an electrical wall heater has been installed. The plumbing is also working, hot water included.

On our every-other-week Costco run, I discovered Costco had mattresses on sale, so started my home spending by buying a mattress.

And now I'm painting, because I'm pretty sure I can live in a space that's 108 square feet. But I'm pretty sure I cannot live in a space that's bright orange and green.

APRIL 29, 2020 - ARCATA, CALIFORNIA

This morning I reminded myself to practice happiness as I painted. Awareness, acceptance, appreciation, anticipation.

The first step in practicing happiness is always to take a deep, mindful breath. But my deep breath smelled like paint fumes.

My second step is to check my physical well-being: is there anything that needs fixing that I can easily fix? Is there something I could do to be more comfortable, to feel better? A snack, a sweater, a better arrangement of pillows? A cup of tea, a more pleasant scent from my essential oil diffuser, music more appropriate for my mood?

Given that I was painting, the answer was no. A cup of tea might have been nice, but I wasn't going to take a break for it. I would accept where I was, although I felt more grumpy and resigned than actually accepting.

The next step is appreciation. I start with gratitude, thinking of something I'm grateful for. That's easy right now, of course, because the world is a terrifying mess, but being grateful not to have bad things happening to me or those I love is not a good kind of gratitude. It doesn't make me happy, it makes me anxious.

But when practicing happiness, appreciation is also of the moment: I look for something delightful. Maybe it's something purely beautiful, like the rhododendrons flowering all over the place, or maybe it's charming, like the chickens or the sleeping cats. A sound, a smell, a sight.

In a national forest, it's easy to find something to appreciate. In this case, I was staring at a wall and I'd been staring at the exact same wall for four mornings in a row. It didn't give me a lot of scope for delight.

At that point, I had to laugh at myself. I don't usually fail quite so thoroughly in my happiness practice.

Fortunately, laughing at myself improved my mood and I started working on reframing my task, from an incredibly tedious repetition of yesterday's chore to a careful investment in my long-term future.

I started anticipating, imagining what the Tiniest House would be like when I'd been living in it for a few months, a year, many years? I pictured myself twenty years in the future, still living here. My imaginary Future Me was being grateful to imaginary Past Me for creating such a cozy space, which made Present Me a lot more tolerant of my efforts.

MAY 8, 2020 - ARCATA, CALIFORNIA

My intensive painting days did not last for the three days I expected them to. They lasted forever.

Well, or a week, whichever comes first.

Technically, I'm still not done: my new home is a work in progress. But I've moved into it.

It felt... strange... to be moving out of *Serenity*. Suffice to say, my feelings are complicated.

What a weird time this is.

The other day Suzanne and I were sitting outside on the back patio, enjoying the sunshine and eating something — possibly gluten-free chocolate cupcakes with mint buttercream icing? — and I said, "I'm quite enjoying our apocalypse."

Suzanne's garden

Whenever I'm thinking — about the pandemic, about the economy, about politics, about Zelda's health, about climate change, about the future, about the state of the world — I'm deeply sad and worried.

But whenever I stop thinking and just exist, my life is delightful.

Moral of the story: more existing, less thinking.

JUNE 23, 2020 - ARCATA, CALIFORNIA

Yesterday morning, I woke up in my comfortable, cozy bed, underneath my cotton quilt, with sun shining through my skylight, and I thought, "I have a skylight. And a tiny house. And hot running water, and comfortable pillows, and a snoring dog and a garden... I think I might be a character in a fairy tale."

And then I woke up all the rest of the way and thought, "Fairy tale? Which one?" I don't know the answer to that, but not Hansel and Gretel. Maybe a Robin McKinley book.

I told Suzanne I wanted roses for the strip of garden plot that exists between the patio and the tiny house wall. In another odd moment of serendipity, a house down the street is being knocked down to be replaced by some ugly apartment building. It had a huge, beautiful rose bush that was going to be destroyed, so we wandered down there and asked the guys doing construction if we could take it. They said sure.

Unfortunately, huge, beautiful rose bushes are hard to dig up. But Suzanne took a bunch of clippings and they're sprouting leaves in a glass on the kitchen sink. Someday my tiny house will also have roses.

I'm still struggling not to let the state of the world drag me into despair, still worrying and then trying to remember to breathe and let go.

Practicing happiness has honestly never been harder. But I love my tiny house more every day.

And *Serenity* is parked outside. Someday, maybe even someday soon, we will be back on the road again.

10

AUTHOR'S NOTE

Zelda lived until January 9, 2021. The last six months of her life were filled with beach visits, small adventures, naps in the sunshine, and many, many treats. Although her canine dementia grew increasingly worse and became harder on both of us, she never became aggressive and she never forgot who I was.

I was her person until her very last breath.

She will always be my girl.

When I started turning my blog posts into a book, I thought it was going to be about the practicalities of living in a van. Tips about finding places to camp, managing your water use, washing dishes, staying organized, that kind of thing. I'm not sure I succeeded in that, but I hope if you're considering van life, you found something useful in my words.

If anything I wrote about fear resonated with you, I highly recommend looking into Acceptance and Commitment Therapy. Most therapists these days practice Cognitive-Behavioral Therapy (in part because insurance companies are willing to pay for it.) CBT is about changing the way you think, reframing your understanding of your experience. It's helpful and I'm not disparaging it.

But Acceptance and Commitment Therapy is about learning to live with your feelings, to accept them as they are, and then to move past them into changing your behavior so that it aligns with your values. I don't credit ACT with changing my life — I changed my life — but the tools and techniques I discovered while learning about ACT have made me a happier person.

Over the course of the four years I lived in *Serenity*, I wrote about 350,000 words on my blog and another 1.2 million words or so in my journals. In creating this memoir, I kept the blog format, but used both in telling my story; condensing, merging, and sometimes rearranging.

Obviously, I left a lot out. If you're one of the many, many, many people I met along the way and I didn't share our story, I'm sorry. It doesn't mean it wasn't important to me. Deciding what to include and what to leave out was remarkably difficult.

Now is the moment when a good author thanks all of the people who helped her. I don't even know where to begin. So many people! So many friends, so many family members, so many chance-met acquaintances who shared campfires, advice, meals and sometimes their showers. So much kindness.

And so many names I never knew: the woman at Valley Truck Service in Black Mountain, North Carolina; the boy who bandaged Zelda after the attack; Helpful Guys #1 and #2 in Yellowstone; the grumbling guy who fixed my leaking toilet on Prince Edward Island — not all of your stories made it into this book, but to all of you, and so many more, thank you for enriching my life.

Special thanks, though, and immense gratitude, to my brother, who is the Best Brother Ever and always will be; to Christina Pearson, amazing cook, awesome host, and incredible friend; and to Suzanne Stafford, my shelter in the storm.

ABOUT THE AUTHOR

Sarah Wynde used to live in a camper van named Serenity: exploring new places, appreciating serendipity, and practicing happiness. Now she lives in a tiny house named Serendipity, and she appreciates it very much.

She likes cautious adventures, creative meals, and sunshine. She hates writing and frequently gives it up as an unhealthy addiction. She usually starts again, because daydreaming is more fun when she can share her imaginary worlds with other people.

Her real name is Wendy Sharp. You could have guessed that from the copyright page, but she thought it important to mention. Also, she notes that managing multiple identities is a hassle best avoided.

She's mostly abandoned social media because it doesn't add to the quality of her life, but you really didn't need to get in touch with her anyway, did you?

Made in United States
Orlando, FL
06 June 2023

33857243R00153

Honest and wry, a story about choosing happiness over comfort and living bravely in the face of fear.

In March of 2016, Sarah Wynde decided to sell her house, buy a camper van, and travel the country.

She was a single mom whose son was grown and gone; living in Florida in a house she adored but whose upkeep and maintenance were a constant churn of worry; and she was a little less than gainfully employed.

Nomadland hadn't been published yet, and it would be another year before she learned about the #vanlife movement from *The New Yorker*. Sarah didn't even have an Instagram account.

But her life felt stagnant. She didn't know what she wanted, but she knew she needed something different.

Based on her blog posts and journals, interspersed with some present-day advice on van living and happiness, this is the story of what she did, how she did it, and what she learned along the way.

Sarah Wynde used to live in a camper van named Serenity: exploring new places, appreciating serendipity, and practicing happiness. She likes long walks, cautious adventures, and creative meals. She hates writing and frequently gives it up as an unhealthy addiction. She somehow always starts again, mostly because daydreaming is more fun when she can share her imaginary worlds with other people. This is her first memoir, but she's written and published seven novels.

ISBN 9798714823725

9 798714 823725

9 0 0